Dishes & Beverages of the Old South

Martha McCulloch-Williams

Dishes & Beverages of the Old South

*A facsimile of the original,
published in 1913,
with a new introduction
by John Egerton*

The University of Tennessee Press

KNOXVILLE

Frontispiece: Photograph of Martha McCulloch-Williams made
at J. K. Cole Studio, 174 Sixth Avenue, New York City, in
about 1913, the year she published *Dishes & Beverages of the
Old South*. (Original photograph property of Frances Edwards
Polk of Nashville, Tennessee, great-niece of Martha McCulloch-
Williams.) Decorations in original edition by Russell Crofoot.

Library of Congress Cataloging in Publication Data
McCulloch-Williams, Martha, b. ca. 1857.
  Dishes & beverages of the old South /
  by Martha McCulloch-Williams;
  with a new introduction by John Egerton.
    p.   cm.
  "A facsimile of the original, published in 1913."
  Includes index.
  ISBN 0-87049-580-1 (cloth: alk. paper)
  1. Cookery, American—Southern style. 2. Beverages—Southern
States. 3. Southern States—Social life and customs—1865—
I. Title. II. Title: Dishes and beverages of the old South.
TX715. M474315 1988
641.5973—dc19   88-2981   CIP

Contents

Introduction

The literature of Southern cookery is almost as venerable and as distinctive as the food itself. For nearly two and a half centuries, writers inspired by the creative genius of the region's cooks have been describing the natural and homemade wonders of the table in a flow of words that has gradually increased from a trickle to a torrent. Like the cooks, the writers have also exhibited flashes of originality, together with a spirit of enthusiasm undimmed by repetition. Further, the writers have become almost as prolific as the cooks, turning out recipe collections and specialized cookbooks that rival in number and diversity the productions of the kitchen.

First on the list of cookery volumes emanating from the South was *The Compleat Housewife; or, Accomplish'd Gentlewoman's Companion*, written by E. (for Eliza) Smith and published by William Parks of Williamsburg, Virginia, in 1742. It was, in fact, the first cookbook to be published in this country, and while it was essentially an abridgement of an English volume, it opened the way for the domestic collections that gradually followed.

Mary Randolph, another Virginian, entered the cookbook field in 1824 with *The Virginia House-Wife*, a classic work that food historian Karen Hess has called "the most influential American cookbook of the nineteenth century." Unlike its predecessors, it was not imported but homegrown, showing the influences of Indian and African as well as European traditions in the making of a new American—and Southern— cookery.

The Virginia House-Wife inspired two more Southern volumes of similar content, and even their titles reflected Mrs. Randolph's influence. One was *The Kentucky Housewife* (1839), by Lettice Bryan, and the other was *The Carolina Housewife* (1847), by Sarah Rutledge, writing anonymously as "a lady of Charleston." By mid-century, Southern cooks, writers, and publishers had established themselves as leaders in the American cookbook field, and although they were temporarily silenced by the Civil War, they quickly returned to prominence in the postwar years.

The last three decades of the nineteenth century brought a large number of new Southern cookbooks into print. Almost every state in the region contributed at least one good volume, and some were either written by non-Southerners (for example, *The Dixie Cook-Book*, compiled anonymously by Estelle Woods Wilcox of Ohio) or published in the North (Mrs. A. P. Hill's *New Cook Book* and Mrs. M. E. Porter's *New*

Southern Cookery Book, issued in New York and Philadelphia, respectively).

Southern writers in other fields also contributed volumes on food. Virginia novelist Mary Virginia Hawes Terhune, writing under a pseudonym (Marion Harland), enjoyed great national success with a book called *Common Sense in the Household*, and in New Orleans, journalist Lafcadio Hearn was the anonymous author of a popular volume named *La Cuisine Creole*.

Louisiana and Kentucky led the expanding parade of Southern cookbooks into the twentieth century, Louisiana with the thoroughly detailed and now-classic *Picayune Creole Cook Book* (1900) and Kentucky with two 1904 volumes, *The Blue Grass Cook Book* by Minnie C. Fox and *The Blue Ribbon Cook Book* by Jennie C. Benedict. Eighty years after Mary Randolph created her prototype *House-Wife*, the South's library of cookery books was thriving, with new and better volumes being added almost continuously.

And yet, for all its energetic vitality, the Southern cookbook movement confined a burgeoning diversity of content within a static form. Curiously, the style in which Southerners—and other Americans—delivered their recipes to the reading public didn't change much over the years. In the nineteenth century no less than the eighteenth (and, in fact, even now, as the twentieth draws to a close), the standard method of organization was strictly utilitarian; categories of recipes, some sort of sequential order for the named entries, a list of ingredients and a brief set of instructions for each recipe, and not much else. A certain level of prior knowledge and experience usually was assumed, and little in the way of social or cultural or historical context was given. Recipes simply stood or fell on their own merits, the ultimate test being whether or not a skillful cook could follow them with succesful results.

Unfortunately, this bare-bones approach ages poorly. Contemporary readers of eighteenth-century cookbooks will find in them almost nothing to explain that mango pickles were really melons, or that isinglass was a kind of gelatine made from fish bladders, or that journey cake (some said Johnny cake) was originally a hearth-baked "pocket" bread the early Americans made with corn—imitating their European ancestors, who made it with oatmeal or barley. Recipes alone, with no supporting text, can be as mystifying—and eventually as frustrating—as a set of instructions for assembling a complex piece of machinery.

With these facts of cookbook history to contemplate, the reader may find all the more remarkable the volume here at hand—*Dishes & Beverages of the Old South*—and its author, Martha McCulloch-Williams. She was born and raised on a Tennessee plantation in the antebellum period, and lived there through the Civil War and Reconstruction. Years later, when she was a sixty-five-year-old professional writer residing in New York City, she created from memory a narrative description of the food of her childhood and youth. In the process, she developed a style of writing about food that few if any had tried before her and only a small number have mastered since. Finally, there is this ironic twist to the story: Both the author and her pathfinding book slipped away with the passage of time and disappeared virtually without a trace, leaving other writers to reinvent the wheel of narrative books about food, apparently without the slightest inkling of what had been done before them.

Martha McCulloch-Williams and her *Dishes & Beverages* deserve a better fate, and that is the principal motivation for this facsimile reproduction of the book and these biographical notes on her life.*

She was born in the plantation home of her parents, William Collins and Fannie Williams Collins, near the Tennessee-Kentucky border northwest of Clarksville in 1848. They christened her Susan Martha Ann Collins, and from early on she

---

*Concerning the book, I wish to express my gratitude to Evalin Douglas of Lexington, Kentucky, who first showed me a copy, and to Ann Egerton, whose diligent search finally located one for sale. For

answered to a nickname—Smack—that was both an acronym and a descriptive term for her quick, sharp wit and her independent manner.

As the last of four surviving children (all girls), she benefited not only from the presence of her older sisters but also from the doting attention of her father, a leisure-loving country gentleman in his fifties, and her mother, who was in her mid-thirties. Smack, some said, was a lot like her father.

William Collins was twenty-nine when he moved to Middle Tennessee from Granville County, North Carolina, with his aging parents in 1826. His father, who was descended from six generations of early English settlers in Virginia and the Carolinas, had amassed a fortune in land and slaves by the time he migrated to Tennessee, and the twelve Collins children were in line to inherit the wealth. As one of the eldest males, William came into a substantial fortune. He had already built his own Montgomery County estate adjacent to the family homeplace when his father died in 1838, and as the years passed he was content to let overseers and slaves raise his to-

the information on Martha McCulloch-Williams, I am indebted to Clarksville historian Ursula Smith Beach, who put me on the right trail, to Annette Hale of the Library of Congress, and to Frances Edwards Polk of Nashville, a great-niece of Mrs. Williams, who generously shared genealogical material, family letters, photographs (including the frontispiece portrait), and personal recollections with me.

bacco while he sat on the porch and read. "Squire" Collins was not much of a farmer, his neighbors and even some members of his own family observed; he was better at cards than tobacco, and when he took the crop to New Orleans by riverboat each fall, he generally spent most of his time gambling.

Like so many white Southerners of her generation, Martha Collins grew up with an abundance of contradictions. She was eleven when her last surviving grandparent, Polly Clardy Collins, died in 1859. Her paternal grandparents had been devout Methodists and also members of the wealthy, slaveholding squirearchy; her maternal grandparents, with whom she spent little time, apparently had less of everything (except perhaps religious fervor) in their farming community in a neighboring county. On the Collins plantation, the established pattern of labor dictated that blacks who had nothing did the hard work for whites, who had all that money could buy, and it was to perpetuate that arrangement that Southern whites eventually chose to rebel against their country. The Collinses stood firmly with the rebels.

The family of William and Fannie Collins stayed together through the Civil War, there being no males of fighting age among them, but the conflict claimed the life of elder sister Mary's sweetheart, and she never forgave the Yankees or married anyone else. The war was also at least partially responsible for the fact that Martha never went to school, although she did receive some home instruction in the classics from Mary, who earlier had gone away to study. Another sister, Virginia, married a neighborhood farmer's son named Lewis Edwards right after the war, but the fourth Collins girl, Sarah Gold, remained single, and so the Collins family entered the postwar era with both parents and three grown daughters living together in the big house where all the girls had been born.

For the next twenty years they kept that close family association. The aging parents held on to their land, but they had neither the money nor the manpower to operate the farm at a high level of productivity. In the familiar style of genteel poverty that characterized so many landed white Southerners of that period, they got by on a fraction of their antebellum wealth. A few elderly black retainers stayed with them to do the cooking and perform other services, but there was more form than substance in the family's effort to recapture its privileged past.

It was during these years that Martha began to write regularly for the Clarksville *Leaf-Chronicle*, signing her stories "Smack Collins." She had a distinctive style that readers liked, and as her experience increased, so did her ambition.

In 1885, William Collins died at the age of eighty-eight, and his wife passed away soon thereafter. Meanwhile, a distant cousin, Thomas McCulloch Williams—a relative from Fannie

Collins's side of the family—had moved into the house to help shoulder some of the responsibility, and he stayed on with the three unmarried sisters after the passing of their parents. That was enough in those strait-laced times to set tongues to wagging throughout the rural community, but it was not the least Collins act to trouble the neighbors, nor would it be the last. In fact, Martha's notoriety was just beginning.

She was thirty-seven the year her father died—eleven years younger than Mary, six younger than Gold—and by far the most outgoing and unconventional. She wanted to take over as manager of the family farm, but the others didn't like that idea, and they couldn't agree on a satisfactory arrangement. Finally, in 1887, they decided to sell the property. Mary and Gold went to live with sister Virginia and her family on their farm nearby. Martha, to the consternation of one and all, decided to leave Montgomery County and move to New York to seek her fortune as a writer—and Thomas McCulloch Williams, the distant cousin who apparently had become her intimate companion, went with her. She was almost forty, and he was a few years older, but social custom made no allowances for such out-of-wedlock pairings at any age. Martha's sisters were stung by the embarrassment and scandal of it all.

Smack Collins left her nickname, her maiden name, and her Tennessee country ways behind and threw herself wholeheartedly into the center of an urban writer's way of life. Tall and attractive and very bright, she was brimming with energy and confidence, and before long she was picking up magazine assignments with regularity. She adopted a new by-line, calling herself Martha McCulloch-Williams—very British, even down to the hyphen, which she apparently threw in purely for effect. She wrote Victorian short stories and serials, poetry, and essays on nature for several magazines, including *Harper's Monthly, Harper's Bazaar,* and *McClure's,* and in 1892 her first book, *Field Farings* ("a vagrant chronicle of earth and sky"), was published by Harper & Brothers. Within a decade, three more of her books were in print (*Milre, Two of a Trade, Next to the Ground*) and she was securely established as a minor but by no means invisible member of the New York literary community. It was a status she relished.

Thomas, too, was thoroughly satisfied with life in the big city. Martha's share of her father's estate and her earnings from writing were enough for the two of them to live comfortably on Amsterdam Avenue on Manhattan's Upper West Side, and Thomas seemed content to leave the ambitious striving and hard work to her. Whether or not they ever married is not entirely clear; in any case, they had no children, and thus Martha was free to give her undivided attention to writing. The result was a prolific outpouring of stories, articles, and books.

It might seem on the surface that Martha McCulloch-

Williams never looked back to Tennessee from her literary perch in New York, but that was not the case. She maintained close contact with her sisters (who, after the death of Virginia's husband, moved to Hopkinsville, Kentucky, to live with a relative), and she went occasionally to visit them, even though Thomas never went with her. Further, she kept her Southern accent throughout her life, and with it a devotion to Old South ways. And, her books and stories generally drew upon Southern scenes and settings. Writing in a period when it was popular and fashionable (in New York as well as in Nashville or New Orleans) to indulge in sad laments over the "lost cause" of the Confederacy and to romanticize and glorify the Southern past, the old Smack Collins occasionally lapsed into flashes of Rebel defiance. For the most part, however, she was content to pen wistful, sometimes humorous, and always well-written descriptions of what she remembered as "the good old days."

In view of her loyalty to the social code of the Old South, it must have galled Martha Collins Williams that her reputation as a writer was fairly well established in Yankeeland but virtually nonexistent back home. She was a product of *noblesse oblige* paternalism and what might be called benevolent white supremacy; she sang the praises of her resident "Aunt Jemima" and "Uncle Tom" servants on the plantation (calling them, without a trace of intended irony, "Mammy and Black Daddy"). Still, it was readers in the North who bought her work, while in the South, where her sentiments were not at all uncommon, her writing was not widely known or appreciated.

Another of her personal traits that seems typically Southern was her eccentricity. The South has always prided itself on its local characters. Martha certainly seemed to fit the description; in fact, she nourished her reputation for offbeat behavior. When her beloved Thomas died in the first decade of the twentieth century, ending their sojourn of twenty years together in New York, she brought his ashes back to Tennessee in a little wooden box—and over the strenuous objections of her sisters, she insisted on appearing with his remains at the dinner table and placing them in the chair next to her. She also did her knitting on Sunday while the others went to church, cooked with (and sometimes nipped on) alcoholic beverages, and delighted in a good off-color joke, whether someone else's on her own.

Clarksville and Montgomery County (and later Hopkinsville, across the line in Kentucky) never seemed to decide just how to react to this local girl turned glamorous New York literary figure. More than anything else, they simply ignored her. After Thomas Williams died and Martha had deposited his ashes in the Tennessee soil, she returned to Manhattan to take up writing again. Her career was on the wane, and it appeared for a while that she would never write another book.

But then, when she was sixty-five years old, a remarkable

thing happened. Quite unexpectedly, she produced what then and now must be considered her best work. It was published in 1913 by McBride, Nast & Company, a highly-regarded New York house, and it introduced a new method of writing about food. Drawing from memory upon the cookery and kitchen lore of her childhood, Martha McCulloch-Williams wrote a narrative treatment of the subject that apparently was untried before her—and it would be decades before anyone improved upon it. In its time it was a little gem, and it still is. This is that book: *Dishes & Beverages of the Old South.*

———————

The novel idea that Martha McCulloch-Williams brought to her *magnum opus* was disarmingly simple. The subject was food in her native South, and some recipes would be absolutely essential to the task, but this was not to be a cookbook in any conventional sense. Instead, it would be a connected series of essays—stories—describing people and events in a specific time and place. The finished manuscript was nearly 50,000 words long and was organized into fifteen chapters that began with "Grace Before Meat" and ended with "Soap and Candles," but followed no strongly logical sequence along the way. About two hundred recipes were discreetly tucked into the prose and indexed in the back of the book, the latter being the only obvious concession to cookbook orthodoxy.

In the very first paragraph, Mrs. Williams displayed the highly personal, conversational, assertive style that she would sustain throughout. "Proper dinners means so much—good blood, good health, good judgment, good conduct," she declared. Miserable dinners, on the other hand, may cause all manner of troubles, from dyspepsia to defeat in war. "It is said," she wrote, that "underdone mutton cost Napoleon the battle of Leipsic, and eventually his crown. I wonder, now and then, if the prevalence of divorce has any connection with the decline of home cooking?"

It is not hard to imagine the author reading over her opening lines and chuckling with delight. Did she mean to be deadly serious, or mildly outrageous, or entertainingly humorous? We can't be certain—perhaps all three. In any case, the effect was attention-grabbing. She pressed on:

"A far cry, and heretical, do you say, gentle reader? Not so far after all—these be sociologic days. I am but leading up to the theory with facts behind it, that it was through being the best fed people in the world, we of the South Country were able to put up the best fight in history, and after the ravages and ruin of civil war, come again to our own. We might have been utterly crushed but for our proud and pampered stomachs, which in turn gave the bone, brain and brawn for the conquests of peace. So here's to our Mammys—God bless them! God rest them! This imperfect chronicle of the nurture wherewith they fed us is inscribed with love to their memory."

In just two pages, she praised the virtues of Southern cookery, explained the fall of Napoleon, revealed what kept the South in a fight it was doomed to lose, and honored the black women whose kitchen wisdom she admired so deeply. It was a marvelous mixture of doubtful history, shaky sociology, marginal logic, good instincts, and superb writing. Whatever faults she had, she knew how to hook her readers and pull them into her narrative, and to keep them there, turning pages and exclaiming.

Her descriptive powers were remarkable. Although she was twenty-five years removed from daily life on the plantation and more than fifty years distant from the antebellum scenes she was describing, her carefully detailed accounts were clear and authentic and altogether believable. Memory-walking through the separate kitchen that stood in the yard behind the big house, she catalogued the pots and skillets and utensils of open-hearth cookery and proclaimed the method to be superior to woodstove cooking (not to mention gas or electricity). Her antebellum kitchen could have been colonial, as pertinent to 1650 as 1850, and few if any have ever been more extensively documented.

Viewed from a 1980s perspective, Mrs. Williams's words

about the black woman she called "Mammy" are hopelessly condescending and degrading. She is credited with no name except Mammy; she is described and quoted in such a way as to suggest ridicule, and her inferior status is made clear even as she is proclaimed to be "autocratic" and "a benevolent despot" in the kitchen. Still, the subtle complexities of the relationship between Mammy the woman and Martha the child are also a part of this story, and sometimes they are exposed with revealing clarity. For example, there is never a mention of anyone white who is an important teacher in this child's eyes; it is from Mammy and other blacks that she gets stories, proverbs, songs, and news from the countryside—in short, "a liberal education in the humanities." And it is specifically and exclusively from Mammy that she learns "how things ought to taste," and declares that this knowledge "has been the polestar of my career as a cook."

For all her antebellum airs, Martha McCulloch-Williams was in many ways a thoroughly modern cook and writer and thinker, a woman ahead of her time. She disliked "over-elaboration" and pretentiousness. "Enough of one thoroughly good thing," she declared, could be "more satisfying than seven courses." On the right occasion, she said, "the one-piece dinner is as convenient and comfortable as the one-piece frock." She described herself as an "ardent advocate of temperance," but added in the same breath, "I refused to consider writing this book unless I had full liberty to advise the use of wine, brandy, cordials, liquors where good cooking demands them." Julia Child probably would have sat reverently at her feet, taking copious notes.

On the subject of cornbread, Mrs. Williams began by warning that "the cornmeal of commerce will not be satisfactory in any receipt here given." For flavor, she said, nothing could beat water-ground meal made from white flint corn—and now, almost seventy-five years later, the statement is still true. Her biscuits, salt-rising bread, egg bread, cracklin' bread, and batter cakes also stand the test of time. And here as elsewhere throughout the book, it is the writing as much as the recipes themselves that is so compelling.

The chapter called "Saving Your Bacon" begins with a classic account of hog-killing, "a festival as joyous as Christmas—and little less sacred." Through twenty pages of the most precise and detailed description, the process and the foodstuffs yielded from it stand out with such clarity that you are led to wonder if this upper-class woman long gone from the farm has by some improbable arrangement managed just now to perform this strenuous and bloody task herself. She knows every step, from the slaughter to the sausage, and she leads her readers relentlessly onward until nothing is left but hair and bone. Salt-cured, smokehouse-aged country hams are the most prized products of a hog-killing, and Martha Williams lingers over them. Her method of cooking such a ham is involved, elaborate, fussy—in fact, bordering on endless and seemingly out of character for her—but in perspective it still makes interesting reading.

The beverages of *Dishes & Beverages* are essentially alcoholic, from cherry bounce (a fruit and whiskey liqueur) through persimmon beer and eggnog and blackberry cordial to several kinds of fruit wine, including gooseberry and muscadine. Mrs. Williams may have approved of temperance in the narrow and literal meaning of the term, but she apparently didn't encourage abstinence.

In the chapter on pastry, pies, and puddings, the author gives us her "philosophy of pie crust," and says of more complicated puff paste that cooks should "beware undertaking it until you have experience or the confidence of absolute ignorance for your help." Her own array of cobblers, fried pies, cream pies, cheesecakes, custards, and puddings is hunger-inducing, and her cakes, though old-fashioned in a contemporary perspective, are nonetheless diverse and appealing.

There is an essay on Creole cookery, based mainly on the everyday masterpieces of a New Orleans cook named Milly who worked for a time in New York. "She did not make friends readily," Mrs. Williams wrote, "but the comradery of cooking induced her to more than tolerate me." What Milly taught Martha would still be superlative in New Orleans today.

Meat, poultry, game, and egg dishes make up another category of Williams specialties, and here she serves a balanced mixture of standard and unusual recipes: barbecued lamb, beefsteak with bacon and onions, roast turkey and stuffing, guinea hen in casserole, fried chicken and gravy, poultry hash, smothered rabbit or squirrel, wild duck, roasted possum. On eggs she is eloquent; among the dishes are potato egg puffs, egg dumplings, poached eggs topped with a lemon-butter sauce, and something called egg fours (topped with sardines, olives, pimento, and seasonings). She closes with the simplest method of all. "Anybody, almost, can fry an egg wrong," she declares. "It takes some skill to fry one exactly right." She proceeds to tell you how, as you've probably never heard the method described before.

The soups and salads and relishes seem old-fashioned, yet somehow quite modern. There is black turtle bean soup, as served today in Florida's Spanish restaurants, and gumbo (à la Creole Louisiana); there is wedding salad (better known now as chicken salad), and "cold" slaw; there is spiced grapes, a jelly-like sauce for meat or bread. Mrs. Williams obviously liked to use fruits in a variety of ways; among the unusual concoctions she describes here are cherries piquant (a highly spiced all-purpose sauce), "apple sauce gone to heaven" (really a baked apple dish), sweet-sour pears, spiced plums, and baked peaches.

With her innate sense of good cookery, Martha Williams demonstrates again and again that she knows how to combine simple things in order to make her food taste good. She has absorbed through her pores the lessons of her mentors, and in spite of her long absence from the Southern scene, she still carries the wisdom with her. And best of all, she also knows how to tell complex stories in clear and simple language.

Her vegetable recipes mark her as a true Southerner in her kitchen leanings—if, indeed, there was ever any doubt. She offers corn pudding, fried corn (in bacon grease), lye hominy (also called samp and hulled corn), candied sweet potatoes, cauliflower au gratin, baked bananas, and green beans cooked with "streaky bacon" or salt pork. Cabbage and greens she cooks the same way, and saves the pot liquor, "a good and cheap substitute for soup on cold days." You can't get much more Southern in the kitchen than with vegetable recipes such as these. (Missing, though, is any mention of grits.)

Mrs. Williams offers a treatise on sandwich-making and another on pickling, including what many an early American cookbook called mangoes—not the tropical fruit but bell peppers, melons, and other fruits and vegetables hollowed out, immersed in vinegar, and then stuffed with highly seasoned cabbage, celery, and other chopped vegetables. For reasons unexplained, recipes for tea, coffee, and chocolate drinks are grouped with the pickles and preserves. Tea (hot, not iced, this being before the widespread Southern popularity of iced tea) is served with rum and lemon. Coffee is made freshly ground. "I always feel that I taste my coffee mostly with my nose," she says. "Nothing refreshes me like the clean, keen fragrance of it—especially after broken rest." Of hot chocolate she says: "I make it only on occasions of high state. Yet—I am said to make it well. Perhaps the secret lies in the brandy—a scant teaspoonful for each cake of chocolate grated," not for flavor but "to give a smoothness to the blending."

Next there is an essay in praise of the peach season, and of apples, watermelons, and quince, an ancient and popular (but now rare) fruit used primarily for jelly-making. And finally, just before the closing instructions on soap and candle making, there is a fascinating chapter called "Upon Occasions."

Here is the climax to any special occasion—and to the Williams book. The very best that hosts and hostesses and cooks have to offer is laid out on these occasions for an assembly of family and friends. There is the infare, a pre-wedding feast paid for by the groom's family to honor the bride, and this is answered by the post-wedding supper, at which the bride's family returns the compliment. Turkey and aged ham are the standby meats, and there is barbecue on some evenings. Often these were stand-up buffet dinners, with plenty of servants to whisk away the used plates and glasses. And next morning there would be turkey hash or thin-sliced ham served on hot biscuits or egg bread.

Party suppers come in every season, often with no excuse for them except the common desire to meet and eat, or simply to keep from wasting food. "There was little luxury," Martha Williams explained. "Rather we lived amid a spare abundance, eating up what had no market." She recalled times when country-fresh eggs "fetched five cents for two dozen," and broiler-size chickens "were forty to fifty cents the dozen." With so much of everything available but not saleable, she said, "stinting would have been sinful." Those pre–Civil War times of abundant foodstuffs were seldom seen again after the war.

And then there is her description of a barbecue—an event, not a pork shoulder. The entire feast is tantalizingly told in six pages of positive prose, including instructions for "barbecue edible" (meat and sauce-making) as distinct from "barbecue, the occasion." Here is some of Mrs. Williams's best writing, as timeless as it is accurate. "A real big barbecue," she wrote, "was a sort of social exchange, drawing together half of three counties, and letting you hear and tell, things new, strange, and startling. . . . To me it seemed as though all the folk in the world had gathered in that shady grove."

Through three hundred pages the food stories of Martha McCulloch-Williams sustain themselves with a smooth, effortless flow, or so it seems; it is easy to imagine that she might have produced a book twice as long and still not run out of tales to tell or recipes to relate. As one of the first—and perhaps the very first—food books of its kind, her narrative stands as a worthy model for newer works that have explored the form, particularly in the past quarter-century. M. F. K. Fisher, Elizabeth David, James Beard, Waverly Root, Eugene Walter, Peter Feibleman and others who have produced distinctive food narratives in recent years must have been inspired by *Dishes & Beverages of the Old South*. Surely they studied it carefully, and gained ideas from it, and sang songs of praise and thanks to the Tennessee-born New Yorker who brought it to life.

Or could it be, ironically, that this first-of-a-kind volume had already disappeared in obscurity by the time they came along, leaving the modern writers to labor in the dark, as it were, not knowing that there was a candle at hand to help them light the way?

———

Little gem though it was, *Dishes & Beverages of the Old South* had a short life in the marketplace. McBride, Nast & Company, its publisher, is no longer in business, and thus the book's sales history is no longer accessible. It seems safe to guess, however, that there was only one printing, probably numbering no more than 3,000 copies. Within a few months after its 1913 appearance in the bookstores, *Dishes & Beverages* had faded into obscurity, and its author seemed to fade with it. She was then sixty-five years old and widowed, living alone in Manhattan. Another of her books also came out in 1913 (*Harper's Household Handbook*, "a guide to easy ways of doing a woman's work," published by Harper & Brothers), but it, too, received only passing notice, and these were to be the last of Martha McCulloch-Williams's career volumes.

She made a few more trips to the Clarksville-Hopkinsville area to visit relatives—particularly her three sisters, who lived together in Hopkinsville—and there remained a fondness among them that transcended past hurts. To all who knew her, Martha remained a good-humored, talkative person, friendly and unpretentious and yet having about her an aura of glamour. Keenly interested in family history and genealogy, she entertained those around her with witty conversation. She also delighted in feeding them from her great repertoire of Southern and exotic dishes.

The four Collins women called one another Sister, and Martha was forever the baby who could be forgiven anything. When others outside the family circle disapproved of her way of life, the elder siblings found the grace to defend her. They forgave her for the old arguments over the family homeplace, for running off with Thomas McCulloch Williams, for working on Sunday, for cooking with whiskey (and drinking it), for telling dirty jokes, for giving up organized religion—and even for bringing Tom's ashes to the dinner table. She sent them newspapers, magazines, and books from New York with her name in them, and they were proud to claim her.

Sister Virginia passed away in 1919 and both Sister Mary and Sister Gold died the following year, leaving Martha as the last surviving member of her generation. She stayed in New York after that, keeping in touch with a few nieces and cousins by mail but never returning to the South. The last years of her life were lonely and unhappy. A fire destroyed her Manhattan home and all her belongings, and then she broke her hip in a fall and ended up in a New Jersey nursing home, where she died at the age of eighty-six in 1934.

One of her closest New York friends for more than a quarter of a century was another Montgomery County native who "made good" as a writer. Her name was Elizabeth Meriwether Gilmer, but she was known professionally as Dorothy Dix (a name she adopted out of respect and admiration for the nineteenth-century social reformer, Dorothea Dix), and she achieved considerable fame and even some fortune as an advice columnist, a precursor of Ann Landers and Abigail Van Buren. As Martha McCulloch-Williams's modest star was in descent, Dorothy Dix's was rising, and it was destined to climb much higher.

It is thus all the more to Dorothy Dix's credit that she found the time to take a personal interest in her failing friend, and eventually to assume full responsibility for her. Soon after Mrs. Williams died in 1934, Dorothy Dix wrote to a member of the family back in Tennessee to "tell you about Mrs. Williams' last days." It was a poignant tale:

> You know some 20 years ago she came to the place, as all writers do at last, where she lost the ability to write articles that the editors would buy. She tried heartbreakingly to do so, but she could not get anything accepted. The something that had made her work good was just gone. Although she had made a living, she had never made enough to save up anything, so she was left destitute, and ever since that time Mrs. Theodosia Garrison Faulks and myself have supported her. . . . I am glad to know that she never wanted for anything. . . .
>
> She had asked Mrs. Faulks, who lived near her, to have her body cremated and the ashes sprinkled in the garden of the cemetery, which was done. There was a nice funeral service with a minister, which I think would have made Martha furious if she had known it, but so it was.
>
> All of the expenses were paid out of a little fund that we had accumulated, so that is settled. She had nothing left but a few clothes and many manuscripts. . . . And so ended a life that was full of bravery and tragedy.

Now, fifty-four years after her death, this reissue of Martha McCulloch-Williams's finest work is a tribute to her originality, her character, and her skill. People in her native Montgomery County, in Tennessee and Kentucky, in the South, and in the nation at large can profit from discovering this talented writer who labored in obscurity to create a sparkling gift for us all. She may have had nothing left when she died, but she left us a culinary and literary treasure, and it is pleasing to know that the long-lost book is finally available once more.

John Egerton
Nashville, Tennessee
March 1988

Dishes & Beverages of the Old South

Grace before Meat

"Let me cook the dinners of a nation, and I shall not care who makes its laws." Women, if they did but know it, might well thus paraphrase a famous saying. Proper dinners mean so much—good blood, good health, good judgment, good conduct. The fact makes tragic a truth too little regarded; namely, that while bad cooking can ruin the very best of raw foodstuffs, all the arts of all the cooks in the world can do no more than palliate things stale, flat and unprofitable. To buy such things is waste, instead of economy. Food must satisfy the palate else it will never truly satisfy the stomach.

9

An unsatisfied stomach, or one overworked by having to wrestle with food which has bulk out of all proportion to flavor, too often makes its vengeful protest in dyspepsia. It is said underdone mutton cost Napoleon the battle of Leipsic, and eventually his crown. I wonder, now and then, if the prevalence of divorce has any connection with the decline of home cooking?

A far cry, and heretical, do you say, gentle reader? Not so far after all— these be sociologic days. I am but leading up to the theory with facts behind it, that it was through being the best fed people in the world, we of the South Country were able to put up the best fight in history, and after the ravages and ruin of civil war, come again to our own. We might have been utterly crushed but for our proud and pampered stomachs, which in turn gave the bone, brain and brawn for the conquests of peace. So here's to our Mammys— God bless them! God rest them! This imperfect chronicle of the nurture wherewith they fed us is inscribed with love to their memory.

Almost my earliest memory is of Mammy's kitchen. Permission to loiter there was a Reward of Merit—a sort of domestic Victoria Cross. If, when company came to spend the day, I made my manners prettily, I might see all the delightful hurley-burley of dinner-cooking. My seat was the biscuit block, a section of tree-trunk at least three feet across, and waist-high. Mammy set me upon it, but first covered it with her clean apron—it was almost the only use she ever made of the apron. The block stood well out of the way—next the meal barrel in the corner behind the door, and hard by the Short Shelf, sacred to cake and piemaking, as the Long Shelf beneath the window was given over to the three water buckets— cedar with brass hoops always shining like gold—the piggin, also of cedar, the cornbread tray, and the cup-noggin. Above, the log wall bristled with knives of varying edge, stuck in the cracks; with nails whereon hung flesh-forks, spoons, ladles, skimmers. These were for the most part hand-wrought, by the local blacksmith.

The forks in particular were of a classic grace—so much so that when, in looking through my big sister's mythology I came upon a picture of Neptune with his trident, I called it his flesh-fork, and asked if he were about to take up meat with it, from the waves boiling about his feet.

The kitchen proper would give Domestic Science heart failure, yet it must have been altogether sanitary. Nothing about it was tight enough to harbor a self-respecting germ. It was the rise of twenty feet square, built stoutly of hewn logs, with a sharply pitched board roof, a movable loft, a plank floor boasting inch-wide cracks, a door, two windows and a fireplace that took up a full half of one end. In front of the fireplace stretched a rough stone hearth, a yard in depth. Sundry and several cranes swung against the chimney-breast. When fully in commission they held pots enough to cook for a regiment. The pots themselves, of cast iron, with close-fitting tops, ran from two to ten gallons in capacity, had rounded bottoms with three pertly outstanding legs, and ears either side for the iron pot-hooks, which varied in size even as did the pots themselves.

Additionally there were ovens, deep and shallow, spiders, skillets, a couple of teakettles, a stew kettle, a broiler with a long spider-legged trivet to rest on, a hoebaker, a biscuit-baker, and waffle-irons with legs like tongs. Each piece of hollow ware had its lid, with eye on top for lifting off with the hooks. Live coals, spread on hearth and lids, did the cooking. To furnish them there was a wrought iron shovel, so big and heavy nobody but Mammy herself could wield it properly. Emptied vessels were turned upside down on the floor under the Long Shelf—grease kept away rust. But before one was used it had to be scoured with soap and sand rock, rinsed and scalded. Periodically every piece was burned out—turned upside down over a roaring fire and left there until red hot, then slowly cooled. This burning out left a fine smooth surface after scouring. Cast iron, being in a degree porous, necessarily took up traces of food when it had been used for cooking a month or so.

Ah me! What savors, what flavors came out of the pots! Years on years I was laughed at for maintaining that no range ever turned out things to equal open-hearth cookery. But it took paper bags to prove beyond cavil the truth of my contention. Even paper-bagging does not quite match the open-hearth process, though there is the same secret of superiority, namely, cooking things in their own essence by the agency of hot air. The sealed and loaded bag needs must be laid on a grate-shelf in a hot oven—touch of solid hot iron is fatal to it.

Iron vessels set above smoothly spread coals got hot, but not red-hot—red heat belonged to the lids. They were swung over the fire and heated before setting them in place—then the blanket of coals and embers held in heat which, radiating downward, made the cooking even. Scorching of course was possible unless the cook knew her business, and minded it

well. Our Mammys not only knew their
business but loved it—often with a devotion that raised it to the rank of Art.   Add
the palate of a *gourmet* born, a free hand
at the fat, the sweet, strong waters and
high flavors—what wonder it is to envy
those of us they fed!

My individual Mammy was in figure an
oblate spheroid—she stood five feet, one
inch high, weighed two hundred and fifty
pounds, had a head so flat buckets sat on
it as of right, was as light on her feet, in
number twelve shoes, as the slimmest of
her children and foster children, could
shame the best man on the place at lifting
with the hand-stick, or chop him to a stand-
still—if her axe exactly suited her.   She
loved her work, her mistress, her children
black and white—even me, though I was
something of a trial—her garden and her
God.   All these she served fondly, faithfully, with rare good humor and the nicest
judgment.   Fall soft upon her, rain and
snow!   Sunshine and green grass, make
happy always the slope where she rests!

She put on a clean white frock every

morning—by breakfast time it was a sickly
gray along the front—the thick of the din-
ner-battle was writ large on it in black
smudges.   She herself explained: ''I
ain't sech er dirty 'ooman—hit's dest I'se
so big, dirt ketches me comin' and gwine.''
Air and more air she would have, regard-
less of weather. The big board-window
had its shutter up all day long—-the glass
window was a vexation, since it opened
only halfway. By way of evenning things,
daubing and chinking got knocked out of
at least half the cracks between the wall
logs as sure as Easter came—not to be re-
placed until the week before Christmas.
I doubt if they would have been put back
even then, but that Mammy dreaded criti-
cism, from maids and carriage drivers
visiting kinfolk brought with them. Big
yawning cracks in cold weather were in a
way the hall-mark of poor-white cabins.
It would have half broken Mammy's heart
to give anybody room to say she belonged
to less than real quality.

She was autocratic; a benevolent despot;
withal severe. If I displeased her by

meddling, putting small grimy fingers into pies they should not touch, she set me to shelling black-eyed peas—a task my soul loathed, likewise the meddlesome fingers— still I knew better than to sulk or whine over it. For that I would have been sent back into the house. The kitchen stood thirty yards away from the back door, with a branchy oak in front of it, and another, even branchier, shading the log foot-way between. The house offered only grown-up talk, which rarely interested me. In the kitchen I caught scraps of Brer Rabbit's history, pithily applied, other scraps of song—Mammy always "gave out" the words to herself before singing them— proverbs and sayings such as "Cow want her tail agin in fly-time" applied to an ingrate, or: "Dat's er high kick fer er low horse," by way of setting properly in place a pretender.

Best of all, I got the latest news of the countryside for ten miles around. Wireless has little on the way things ran about among the plantations. It was a point of honor among the black men to have wives or sweethearts away from home. This meant running about nightly—consequently cross-currents of gossip lively enough to make the yellowest journal turn green with envy. Mammy was a trifle apologetic over having a husband no further off than the next neighbor's. To make up for it, however, the husbands who came to his house lived from three to five miles away—and one of them worked at the mill, hence was a veritable human chronicle. Thus Mammy was able to hold her head up with Susan, her sister, who milked and washed.

Susan might have been called a widow of degrees—she had had three husbands, but only two were living. The last parting was always threatening to end in meeting over again—still that did not hinder her cabin from being the rendezvous of all the likeliest fellows within easy walking range. Naturally she had things to tell—worth hearing whether or no they were true. So also had Phoebe, who was a sort of scullion, fetching in wood and water, gathering vegetables, picking chickens, scouring all things from the big pot to the floor. Shelves were scoured daily, the floor three times a week. This had to be a matter of faith after an hour or so—it certainly did not look it. Sweeping, done three times a day, was largely a matter of form. Phoebe went conscientiously over the uncluttered spaces, and even reached the nose of her broom between pots and ovens, but only coarse trash gathered before the broom—all the rest went through the cracks.

Mammy said Phoebe's news could be believed. "De gal don't know no mo'n ter tell dest whut she done heard." She truly was slow-witted and slow-spoken, but Isham, her step-father, was cook to the Gresham brothers, the beaux of the neighborhood, who kept bachelor's hall. His mother had been their Mammy—hence his inherited privilege of knowing rather more about his young masters than they knew themselves.

Little pitchers have big ears. Set it to the credit of the black folk, they always had regard for the innocence of childhood.

Scandal was merely breathed—not even so
hinted as to arouse curiosity. Foul speech
I never heard from them nor a trace of
profanity. What I did hear was a liberal
education in the humanities—as time
passes I rate more and more highly the
sense of values it fixed in a plastic mind.
I think it must have been because our
Mammys saw all things from the elemental
angle, they were critics so illuminating of
manners and morals.

Here ends reminiscence, set down in hope
it may breed understanding. All I act-
ually learned from Mammy and her cooking was—how things ought to taste. The
which is essential. It has been the pole-star
of my career as a cook. Followed faithfully along the Way of Many Failures,
through a Country of Tribulations, it has
brought me into the haven of knowledge
absolute. If the testimony of empty plates
and smiling guests can establish a fact,
then I am a good cook—though limited. I
profess only to cook the things I care to
cook well. Hence I have set my hand to
this, a real cook's book. Most cook books

are written by folk who cook by hearsay—
it is the fewest number of real cooks who
can write so as not to bewilder the common
or garden variety of mind. The bulk of
what follows has an old-time Southern
foundation, with such frillings as experience approves. To it there will be added
somewhat of Creole cookery, learned and
proved here in New York town by grace
of Milly, the very queen of New Orleans
cooks, temporarily transplanted. Also
sundry and several delectable dishes of
alien origins—some as made in France or
Germany, some from the far Philippines,
but all proved before record. In each case
the source is indicated in the title. Things
my very own, evolved from my inner con-
sciousness, my outer opportunity and en-
vironment, I shall likewise mark personal.

Lastly, but far from leastly, let me make
protest against over-elaboration, alike in
food and the serving thereof. The very
best decoration for a table is something
good in the plates. This is not saying one
should not plan to please the eye no less
than the palate. But ribbon on sandwiches

is an anachronism—so is all the flummery
of silk and laces, doilies and doo-dads that
so often bewilder us. They are unfair to
the food—as hard to live up to as anybody's blue china. I smile even yet, re-
membering my husband's chuckles, after
we had come home from eating delicatessen
chicken off ten-dollar plates, by help of an-
tique silver. Somehow the viands and the
service seemed "out of drawing."

Quoth Heine the cynic: "Woman,
woman! Much must be forgiven thee!
Thou hast loved much—and many." Edi-
bly I love much rather than many. Enough
of one thoroughly good thing, with proper
accessories, is more satisfying than seven
courses—each worse than the last. Also
cheaper, also much less trouble. If time
has any value, the economy of it in dish-
washing alone is worth considering. In
these piping days of rising prices, economy
sounds good, even in the abstract. Add
the concrete fact that you save money as
well as trouble, and the world of cooks may
well sit up and take notice.

The one-piece dinner is as convenient and

comfortable as the one-piece frock. There
are, of course, occasions to which it is un-
suited. One-piece must be understood to
mean the *pièce de resistance*—the backbone of subsistence as it were. A bowl of
rich soup or chowder, with crackers on the
side, a generous helping of well-cooked
meat, with bread or potatoes, and the simplest relishes, or a royally fat pudding
overrun with brandy sauce; each or either
can put it all over a splash of this, a dab
of that, a slab of something else, set lone-
somely on a separate plate and reckoned
a meal—in courses. Courses are all well
enough—they have my warm heart when
they come "in the picture." But when
they are mostly "The substance of things
hoped for, the evidence of things not seen,"
then I would trade them, and gladly, for as
much good bread and butter as appetite
called for.

By way of postscript: being a strict and
ardent advocate of temperance, I refused
to consider writing this book unless I had
full liberty to advise the use of wine,
brandy, cordials, liquors, where good cook-

ing demands them. Any earthly thing can be abused—to teach right use is the best preventive of abuse. Liquors, like everything else, must be good. "Cooking sherry" is as much an abomination as "cooking butter," or "cooking apples." You will never get out of pot or pan anything fundamentally better than what went into it. Cooking is not alchemy; there is no magic in the pot. The whole art and mystery of it is to apply heat and seasoning in such fashion as to make the best, and the most, of such food supplies as your purse permits. Tough meat cannot be cooked tender; tainted meat cannot be cooked sound. It is the same with stale fish, specked or soured fruit, withered vegetables. It pays to educate tradesfolk into understanding that you want the best and only the best of what you buy. If the thing you want, in perfect condition, is beyond your means, take, instead of a lower grade of it, the highest grade of something cheaper. So shall you escape waste of time, effort and substance. Never mind sneers at your simple fare. Remember it was Solomon the Wise who wrote: "Better a dinner of herbs and contentment than a stalled ox, and contention therewith." Paraphrase the last clause into "spoiled ox and ptomaines therewith," and you may keep not only self-respect, but that of the neighbors.

The Staff of Life

Bread, more than almost any other food-stuff, can not be better than what it is made of. Here as elsewhere a bungler can ruin the very best of flour or meal. But the queen of cooks can not make good a fundamental deficiency.

Hence in buying flour look for these things: a slightly creamy cast—dazzling whiteness shows bleaching, as a gray-white, or black specks mean grinding from spoiled grain. The feel should be velvety, with no trace of roughness—roughness means, commonly, mixture with corn. A handful tightly gripped should keep the shape of the hand, and show to a degree

the markings of the palm. A pinch wet
rather stiff, and stretched between thumb
and finger, will show by the length of the
thread it spins richness or poverty in glu-
ten—one of the most valuable food ele-
ments.

The cornmeal of commerce will not be
satisfactory in any receipt here given. It
has been bolted and kiln-dried out of all
natural flavor. Take the trouble to get
meal water-ground, from white flint corn,
and fresh from the mill. Then you will
have something worth spending time and
effort upon—spending them hopefully.
Why, the wisest man can not tell—but
steam-ground meal is of a flavor wholly
unlike that water-ground. The grinding
should be neither too fine nor too coarse.
Bran left in, and sifted out as needed,
helps to save from musting, and to preserve the delicate natural flavor. Fresh
meal, in clean bright tin or glass, or in a
stout paper sack, where it is dry, cool and
airy will keep two months. Hence buy it
judiciously, in proportion to your family's
corn-cake appetite.

It is impossible to give exactly the amount of liquid for any sort of bread-making because the condition of flour and meal varies with weather and keeping. This applies also to sugar—hence the need for intelligence in the use of receipts. In damp muggy weather moisture is absorbed from the atmosphere. Upon a dry day especially if there is much wind, drying out is inevitable. Anything that feels clammy, or that clots, should be dried in a warm, not hot, oven. Heating flour before mixing it, taking care not to scorch it in the least, is one small secret of light bread, biscuit and cake. Flour in a bag may be laid in the sun with advantage. Use judgment in mixing. Note the appearance of what you are making closely—when it turns out extra good, set up that first condition as a standard.

Beaten Biscuit: (Old Style.) Sift a quart of flour into a bowl or tray, add half a teaspoon salt, then cut small into it a teacup of very cold lard. Wet with cold water—ice water is best—into a very stiff dough. Lay on a floured block, or marble slab, and give one hundred strokes with a mallet or rolling pin. Fold afresh as the dough beats thin, dredging in flour if it begins to stick. The end of beating is to distribute air well through the mass, which, expanding by the heat of baking, makes the biscuit light. The dough should be firm, but smooth and very elastic. Roll to half-inch thickness, cut out with a small round cutter, prick lightly all over the top, and bake in steady heat to a delicate brown. Too hot an oven will scorch and blister, too cold an one make the biscuit hard and clammy. Aim for the Irishman's "middle exthrame."

There are sundry machines which do away with beating. It is possible also to avoid it by running the dough, after mixing, several times through a food-chopper. Also beaten biscuit can be closely imitated by making good puff paste, rolling, cutting out, pricking and baking—but rather more quickly than the real thing. All these are expedients for those who live in apartments, where the noise of beating might be held against good neighborhood. Householders, and especially suburban ones, should indulge in the luxury of a block or stone or marble slab—and live happy ever after, if they can but get cooks able and willing to make proper use of it.

Soda Biscuit: (Old Style.) Sift a quart of flour with a heaping teaspoonful of baking soda. Add a good pinch of salt, rub well through lard or butter the size of the fist, then wet with sour milk to a moderately soft dough, roll out, working quickly, cut with small round cutter, set in hot pans, leaving room to swell, and bake in a quick oven just below scorching heat. Handle as lightly as possible all through— this makes flaky biscuit.

By way of variety, roll out thin—less than a half-inch, cut with three-inch cutter, grease lightly on top, and fold along the middle. Let rise on top a hot stove several minutes before putting to bake. By adding an egg, beaten light, with a heaping tablespoonful of sugar to the dough in mixing, these doubled biscuit will be quite unlike the usual sort.

Salt Rising Bread: (As Mammy Made It.) Scald a tablespoonful of sifted corn-meal, and a teaspoonful—heaped—of salt with a pint of boiling water, let stand ten minutes, then stir in, taking care to mix smooth, enough dried and sifted flour to make a thick batter. Damp flour will not rise. The batter should be almost thick enough to hold the mixing spoon upright—but not quite thick enough. Set the mixture in warm water—just as hot as you can bear your hand in. Keep up the heat steadily, but never make too hot—scalding ruins everything. Keep lightly covered, and away from draughts. Look in after an hour—if water has risen on top, stir in more flour. Watch close—in six hours the yeast should be foamy-light. Have ready three quarts of dry sifted flour, make a hole in the center of it, pour in the yeast, add a trifle more salt, a tablespoonful sugar, and half a cup of lard. Work all together to a smooth dough, rinsing out the vessel that has held the yeast, with warm not hot water to finish the mixing. Divide into loaves, put in greased pans, grease lightly over the top, and set to rise, in gentle heat. · When risen bake with steady quick heat. Take from pans hot, and cool between folds of clean cloth, spread upon a rack, or else turn the loaves edgewise upon a clean board, and cover with cheese cloth.

To make supper-rolls, shape some of the dough into balls, brush over. with melted butter, set in a deep pan, just so they do not touch, raise and bake the same as bread. Dough can be saved over for breakfast rolls, by keeping it very cold, and working in at morning, a tiny pinch of soda before shaping the balls.

Sweet Potato Biscuit: (Old Style.) Boil soft two large or four small sweet potatoes, mash smooth while very hot, free of strings and eyes, add a pinch of salt, then rub well through three cups of sifted flour. Rub in also a generous handful of shortening, then wet up soft with two eggs beaten very light, and sweet milk. A little sugar also if you have a sweet tooth—but only a little. Roll to half-inch thickness, cut out with small cutter, lay in warm pan, and bake brown in a quick oven. Soda and buttermilk can take the place of eggs and sweet milk—in which case the sugar is advisable. Mix the soda with the milk—enough to make it foamy, but no more.

Waffles: (Mammy's.) Separate three eggs. Beat yolks and whites very light. Add to the yolks alternately a pint of very rich sweet milk, and handfuls of sifted flour. Enough to make a batter rather thicker than cream. Put in also half a teaspoon—scant—of salt, and half a cup of lard, or lard and butter, melted so it will barely run. Mix well, then add the beaten whites of egg. Have the waffle irons hot but not scorching—grease well with melted lard—the salt in butter will make the batter stick. Cook quickly but take care not to burn. Lay on hot plate—have a pitcher of melted butter to pour on. Lay the second waffle upon the first, butter, and keep hot. It is not safe to begin serving without at least six waffles in plate. This, of course, provided you have several eaters with genuine appetites. Syrup can be passed with the waffles—but it is profanation to drench them with it—strong clear coffee, and broiled chicken are the proper accompaniments at breakfast.

Plain Corn Bread: (The Best.) Sift sound fresh white cornmeal, wet with cold water to a fairly soft dough, shape it by tossing from hand to hand into small pones, and lay them as made into a hot pan well sprinkled with dry meal. The pan should be hot enough to brown the meal without burning it. Make the pones about an inch thick, four inches long, and two and a half broad. Bake quickly, taking care not to scorch, until there is a brown crust top and bottom. For hoe-cakes make the dough a trifle softer, lay it by handfuls upon a hot-meal-sprinkled griddle, taking care the handfuls do not touch. Flatten to half an inch, let brown underneath, then turn, press down and brown the upper side. Do not let yourself be seduced into adding salt—the delight of plain corn-bread is its affinity for fresh butter. It should be eaten drenched with butter of its own melting—the butter laid in the heart of it after splitting pone or hoe-cake.

Salt destroys this fine affinity. It however savors somewhat bread to be eaten butterless. Therefore Mammy always said: "Salt in corn-bread hit does taste so po' white-folks'y." She had little patience with those neighbors of ours who perforce had no butter to their bread.

Egg Bread: (Mammy's.) Beat two eggs very light with a pinch of salt, add two cups sifted cornmeal, then wet with a pint of buttermilk in which a teaspoonful of soda has been dissolved. Stir in a spoonful of shortening, barely melted, mix well, and pour into well greased pans or skillets, cook quickly, till the crust is a good brown, and serve immediately. Or bake in muffin moulds. For delicate stomachs the shortening can be left out, but pans or moulds must be greased extra well. If milk is very sour, make it one-third water—this is better than putting in more soda.

Batter Cakes: (Old Style.) Sift together half-cup flour, cup and a half meal, add pinch of salt, scald with boiling water, stir smooth, then add two eggs well beaten, and thin with sweet milk—it will take about half a pint. Bake by spoonfuls on a hot, well-greased griddle—the batter must run very freely. Serve very hot with fresh sausage, or fried pigs' feet if you would know just how good batter cakes can be.

Ash Cake: (Pioneer.) This is possible only with wood fires—to campers or millionaires. Make dough as for plain bread, but add the least trifle of salt, sweep the hot hearth very clean, pile the dough on it in a flattish mound, cover with big leaves —cabbage leaves will do at a pinch, or even thick clean paper, then pile on embers with coals over them and leave for an hour or more, according to size. Take up, brush off ashes, and break away any cindery bits. Serve with new butter and fresh buttermilk. This was sometimes the sole summer supper of very great families in the old time. Beyond a doubt, ash cake properly cooked has a savory sweetness possible to no other sort of corn bread.

Mush Bread: (Overton Receipt.) To a quart of very thick mush, well salted, add three fresh eggs, breaking them in one after the other, and beating hard between. When smooth add half a cup of rich milk, and half a cup melted butter. Stir hard, then add one teaspoonful baking powder, and bake quickly. Bake in the serving dish as it is too soft for turning out, requiring to be dipped on the plates with a spoon. Hence the name in some mouths: ''Spoon bread.''

Cracklin' Bread: (Pioneer.) Sift a pint of meal, add a pinch of salt, then mix well through a teacup of cracklings—left from rendering lard. Wet up with boiling water, make into small pones, and bake brown in a quick but not scorching oven.

Pumpkin Bread: (Pioneer.) Sift a pint of meal, add salt to season fully, then rub through a large cupful of stewed pumpkin, made very smooth. Add half a cup melted lard, then mix with sweet milk to a fairly stiff dough, make pones, and bake crisp. Mashed sweet potato can be used instead of pumpkin, and cracklings, rubbed very fine in place of lard. Folks curious as to older cookery, can even make persimmon bread, using the pulp of ripe persimmons to mix with the meal—but they will need the patience of Job to free the pulp properly from skin and seed.

Mush Batter Cakes: (For Invalids.) Bring half a pint of water to a bubbling boil in something open, add to it a pinch of salt, then by littles, strew in a cup of sifted meal, stirring it well to avoid lumps. Let cool partly, then cook by small spoonfuls on a hot griddle very lightly greased. Make the spoonfuls brown on both sides, and serve very hot.

Wafers: (For Invalids or Parties.) Rub a cup of lard or butter, through a quart of sifted flour. Butter will give enough salt—with lard add a pinch. Mix with sweet milk, the richer the better, to a smooth dough, not stiff nor soft. Shape into balls the size of a small egg, roll out very thin, prick lightly all over, and bake brown—it will take about five minutes in a quick oven. Cool on cloth and keep dry. Handle delicately—if the wafers are what they should be; they break and crumble at any rough touch.

Saving Your Bacon

Plenty in the smokehouse was the corner-
stone of the old time southern cookery.
Hence hog-killing was a festival as joyous as Christmas—and little less sacred.
There was keen rivalry amongst plantations as to which should show the finest
pen of fattening hogs. Though the plantation force was commonly amply sufficient
for the work of slaughter, owners indulged
their slaves by asking help of each other
—of course returning the favor at need.

A far cry from a cook book, common or
garden variety. Here, it is worth its
space, as explaining in a measure what fol-

lows. Namely full direction for choosing your fatted pig, cutting him up, and making the most of the ultimate results. Choose carcasses between a hundred and seventy-five and a hundred and fifty pounds in weight, of a fresh pinky white hue, free of cuts, scratches, or bruises, the skin scraped clean, and firm, not slimy, to touch, the fat firm and white, the lean a lively purplish pink. Two inches of clear fat over the backbone, and the thick of the ribs should be the limit. Anything more is wasteful—unless there is a great need of lard in the kitchen. The pig should be chilled throughout, but not frozen— freezing injures flavor and texture somewhat, besides preventing the proper quick striking in of salt.

Curing space permitting, it is wise to cut up several pigs at once. The trouble is hardly increased, and the results, especially in saving, very much greater. The head will have been at least half severed in slaughtering. With a very sharp butcher knife, after the pig is laid on the chopping block, cut deeply through the skin, all round, then with a blow or two of the axe sever the head. Next cut through the skin deeply, either side of the back bone. The cuts should be evenly parallel, and about two inches apart. Now turn the pig on his back, part the legs and with the meat axe chop through the ribs, and joints. After chopping, cut the backbone free with the knife, trim off the strip of fat for the lard pile, chop the backbone itself into pieces three to four inches long, until the chine is reached—the part betwixt the shoulder blades with the high spinal processes. Leave the chine intact for smoking, along with the jowls and sausage.

Pull out the leaf-fat—it grows around and over the kidneys. Also pull out the spare ribs, leaving only one or two in the shoulders. This done, chop off feet, then with the knife cut hams and shoulders free from the sides. Trim after cutting out, saving all trimmings for sausage. Save every bit of pure fat for lard. Also cut away the clear fat at the top of the sides, devoting it to the same use. Make clean cuts on the joints—this means a knife often whetted. Trim the hams rather flat, and shape the hip bone neatly. The commercial fashion of cutting away all the upper half of hams is fatal to perfect flavor. Trim shoulders close, unless they are destined to be made into sausage—in that case put them with the other scraps. Sides can either be cut into strips four to five inches wide the long way, after the manner of commercial "breakfast bacon," or left whole throughout their streaky part, cutting away solid fat along the top for lard. Separate the heads at the jaw, leaving the tongue attached to the jowl, and taking care not to cut it. Cut off the snout two inches above the tip, then lay the upper part of the head, skin down, crack the inner bone with the axe, press the broken bones apart, and take out the brains. Jowls are to be salted and smoked—heads are best either simply corned for boiling with cabbage, peas, beans, etc., or made in conjunction with the feet into head-cheese, whose south country name is souse.

Use regular pickling salt—coarse-grained and lively. Spread it an inch thick upon clean wood—a broad shelf, box bottom, or something similar. Rub the meat well over with salt, and then lay it neatly, skin-side down, upon the salt layer, spread more salt on top, and put on another layer of meat. Put sides together, likewise hams and shoulders. Pack as close as possible and fill all crevices with salt. Salt alone will save your bacon, but a teacup of moist sugar well mixed through a water-bucket of salt improves the flavor. Use this on sides, jowls and chines. The joints, hams and shoulders, especially if the shoulders are close-cut, need a trifle more sugar in the salt, also a trifle of salt-peter—say an ounce in fine powder to three gallons of salt. Rub the skin-sides over with plain salt, and lay upon the salt-covered shelf the same as sides. Then take a handful of the mixture and rub it in hard around the bone, then cover the whole cut surface half an inch thick, spread on dry salt for another layer of hams or shoulders, and repeat. Salt the chines lightly—their surface, cut all over, takes up too much salt if permitted. There should be holes or cracks in the bottom to let the dissolved salt drip away; it is best also to have it a foot at least above the floor.

Cover the meat thus in bulk, but not too close, and leave standing a fortnight. The cooler and airier the place it stands in the better—freezing even is not objectionable when the salt begins striking in. But with freezing weather the meat must lie longer in salt. Overhaul it after the first fortnight—that is to say break up the bulk, shake away bloody salt, sweep the bottom clean, and put on fresh salt. But use very little saltpeter on the joints this time—on pain of making them too hard as to their lean. Its use is to give firmness and a handsome clear red color—an overdose of it produces a faintly undesirable flavor. Some famous ham makers, at this second salting, rub the cut sides over lightly with very good molasses, and sprinkle on ground black pepper, before adding new salt. Others rub in a teaspoonful of sugar mixed with pounded red pepper around the bone. But very excellent hams can be made without such excess of painstaking.

Let the meat lie two to four weeks after overhauling, according to the weather. Take up, wipe all over with coarse clean cloth, furnish each piece with a loop of stout twine at least four inches long, and so run through the flesh, tearing out is impossible. Run through the hock of hams, the upper tip of shoulders, the thickest part of sides, the pointed tip of jowls. Jowls may not need to lie so long as bigger pieces, especially if part of their fat has gone to lard. Chines can be hung up in three weeks, and cured with a very light smoking, along with the bags of sausage.

Hang hams highest, shoulders next, then sides, jowls, etc. Leave to drip forty-eight hours unless the weather turns suddenly warm, damp and muggy—in that case start the smoking after a few hours. Smoke from green hickory, sound and bright, is needed for the finest flavor. Lay small logs so they will hug together as they burn, kindle fire along the whole length of them, then smother it with damp, small chips, trash, bark and so on, but take care to have everything sound. Rotten

wood, or that which is water-logged or mil-
dewed, makes rank, ill-smelling smoke.
Take greater care that the logs never blaze
up, also that the meat is high enough to
escape fire-heating. Once it gets hot from
the fire all your trouble will have been for
naught—though it will not be tainted it
will have the same taste and smell—the
degree marking the extent of the heating.

Old southern smokehouses had for the
most part earthen floors, trenched to make
the smoke fires safe. Some had puncheon
floors, with an earthen hearth in the
middle, whereupon was placed a furnace
of loose brick—that could be kicked over
at need, smothering an outbreaking fire.
Still others had big cast iron kettles sunk
in a sort of well in the floor—with a handy
water bucket for quenching fires. Whatever the floor, eternal vigilance was the
price of safe bacon—you looked at the
smokehouse fires first thing in the morning and last at night. They were put out
at sundown, but had a knack of burning
again from some hidden seed of live coal.
Morning smoke could not well be too thick,

provided it smelled right—keen and clean, reminiscent of sylvan fragrance—a thick, acrid smoke that set you sneezing and coughing, was "most tolerable and not to be endured." It was not well to leave the smoke too thick at night—somehow the chill then condensed it. A thin, blue, hot-scented but cool, vapor was the thing to strive for then. There were folk who suggested furnaces—with smoke pipes leading in—ever so much safer they said, withal much less trouble. Why! even the smoke from a cooking stove might be made to answer. But these progressives were heard coldly—the old timers knew in right of tradition and experience, the need of well ventilated smoke.

It gave this present chronicler a feeling of getting home again, to walk through the curing rooms of perhaps the most famous bacon makers in the world, and find them practicing the wisdom of her childhood. Namely using hickory smoke not delivered from furnace pipes but welling up, up, in beautiful wreathy spirals, to reach row on row of hams and flitches—and to be told, by a kind person who did not know she already knew, that their curing was patterned on the old English model—curing in the smoke of great-throated stone hall chimneys. Yes—they had tried pipes—furnaces likewise—but they gave too much heat, did not distribute smoke evenly, besides being almost impossible of regulation. Hence the smoldering hickory that was like a breath from a far past.

Notwithstanding, the chronicler is of opinion that folk who would like to try their hands at bacon making may do it with a fair hope without building regular smoke houses. To such she would say, get a stout hogshead—a sugar hogshead preferable—nail on a board roof to shed water, then set it upon a stout frame at least seven feet above ground. Nail inside it stout cleats, to hold the cross bars for the meat. Hang the meat upon them—but not until the hogshead is in place. Cut a hole in the bottom as big as the top of a large barrel. Working through this hole, arrange the meat, then put below a headless barrel, the top resting against the hogshead-heading, the bottom upon supports of gas pipe, iron, or even piled bricks. Between the supports set an iron vessel— build your hickory smoke-fires in it, smothering them carefully, and letting the smoke, with a sufficiency of air, well up, through barrel, hogshead, etc. Or one might even rig up a smoking hogshead in an attic, providing the chimney were tall enough to cool smoke properly—and lead smoke out to it through a length of drain pipe.

These are but suggestions—the contriving mind will doubtless invent other and better ones. Smoking must go on for five weeks at least. Six will be better, slacking toward the end. But two may be made to answer by the use of what is called "liquid smoke" whose other name is crude pyroligneous acid. A product of wood distillation, it has been proved harmless in use, but use is nevertheless forbidden to commercial makers. The meat, after breaking bulk, is dipped in it three times at fairly brief intervals, hung up, drained, and smoked. From the liquid smoke it will have acquired as much acid saving-grace, as from four weeks of old fashioned smoking.

A smokehouse needs to be kept dark, dry, and cool, also well ventilated. Use fine screen wire over all openings, and make windows very small, with coarse, sleazy crash in the sash rather than glass inside the screens. Darkness prevents or discourages the maggot-fly. To discourage him still further cover the cut sides of hams and shoulders before hanging up with molasses made very thick with ground black pepper. They will not absolutely require canvassing and dipping in whitewash after if the peppering is thorough. But to be on the safe side—canvas and dip. Make the whitewash with a foundation of thick paste—and be sure it covers every thread of the canvas. Hams perfectly cured and canvassed keep indefinitely in the right sort of smokehouse—but there is not much gain in flavor after they are three years old.

In rendering lard try out leaf fat to itself—it yields the very finest. Cut out

the kidneys carefully, and remove any bit
of lean, then pull off the thin inner skin,
and cut up the leaves—into bits about two
inches wide and four long. Wash these
quickly in tepid water, drain on a sieve,
and put over a slow fire in an iron vessel
rather thick bottomed. Add a little cold
water—a cupful to a gallon of cut up fat,
and let cook gently until the lumps of fat
color faintly. Increase heat till there is
a mild bubbling—keep the bubbling steady,
stirring often to make sure no lump of fat
sticks to the pot and scorches, until all
the lumps are crisp brown cracklings.
Bright brown, not dark—if dark the lard
will be slightly colored. Scorching taints
and ruins the whole mass. Strain through
a sieve into a clean tin vessel, newly
scalded and wiped dry. Put the cracklings
into a bag of stout crash, and press hard
between two clean boards, till no more fat
runs from them. A jelly press comes in
handy, but is not essential. If weak, clear
lye, made of green wood ashes, is put in
with the fat instead of water at the begin-

ning, the fat-yield will be greater, and the bulk of cracklings less, also more nearly disintegrated.

Other fat is tried out in the same way, taking care to remove all skin and cut away streaks of lean. Bits with much lean in them had better go to the sausage mill —the right proportion there is two pounds of fat to three and a half of lean. Mix well in grinding, and remove all strings, gristle, etc. Seasoning is so much a matter of taste, do it very lightly at first— then fry a tiny cake, test it, and add whatever it seems to lack or need. Be rather sparing of salt—eaters can put it in but can not take it out, and excess of it makes even new sausage taste old. A good combination of flavors, one approved by experience, is a cupful of powdered and sifted sage, an ounce of black pepper newly ground, and very fine, a tablespoonful of powdered red pepper, a teaspoonful of cayenne, a pinch of thyme in fine powder, a dozen cloves, as many grains of alspice, beaten fine, a teaspoonful of moist sugar, and a blade of mace in fine powder. Omit the mace, cloves, etc. if the flavor repels. Mix all well together, then work evenly through the meat. This seasoning should suffice for five pounds of ground meat lightly salted. More can be used by those who like high and pronounced flavors.

Scrape feet very clean, and take off hoofs by either dipping in scalding hot lye, or hot wet wood ashes. Wash very clean after scraping, throw in cold water, soak an hour, then put in a clean pot with plenty of cold water, and boil gently until very tender. If boiling for souse cook till the meat and gristle fall from the bones. If for frying, take up the feet as soon as they are tender, keeping them in shape. Boil heads the same way, taking out eyes, cutting off ears and cleaning them carefully inside. Pick the meat from the bones, mix it with the feet also picked up, work seasoning well through it—salt, black and red pepper, herbs if approved, likewise a trifle of onion juice, then pack in deep molds, pour over a little of the boiling liquor—barely enough to moisten—and set to cool uncovered.

Let the boiling liquor stand until cold, covered only with a cloth. Skim off the oil—hog's foot oil is a fine dressing for any sort of leather—then dip off carefully the jelly underneath. Do not disturb the sediment—take only the clear jelly. Melted, clarified with white of egg, seasoned with wine, lemon juice, or grape juice, and sufficiently sugared, the result puts all gelatines of commerce clean out of court. Indeed any receipt for gelatine desserts can be used with the hog's foot jelly. A small salvage perhaps—but worth while.

Everybody knows brains can be fried— just as all know they can be addled. We of the old south pickled ours. Go and do likewise if you want an experience. Begin by scalding the brains—putting them on in cold water very slightly salted, then letting them barely strike a boil. Skim out, drop in cold water, take off the skin, keeping the lobes as whole as possible, lay in a porcelain kettle, spice liberally with black and red pepper, cloves, nutmeg and allspice, cover with strong vinegar, bring to a boil, cook five minutes, then put in a jar, cool uncovered, tie down and let stand a week before using. Thus treated brains will keep for six weeks, provided they are kept cool.

We also pickled our souse—cutting it in thin slices, and laying them in strong vinegar an hour before serving. Another way was to melt the souse into a sort of rich hash—beaten eggs were occasionally added, and the result served on hot toast. At a pinch it answered for the foundation of a meat pie, putting in with it in layers, sliced hard boiled eggs, sliced cucumber pickle, plenty of seasoning, a good lump of butter, and a little water. The pie was baked quickly—and made a very good supper dish if unexpected company overran the supply of sausage or chicken for frying.

But fried hog's feet were nearly the best of hog killing. After boiling tender, the feet were split lengthwise in half, rolled in sifted cornmeal, salted and peppered, and fried crisp in plenty of boiling hot fat. Served with hot biscuit, and stewed sun-dried peaches, along with strong coffee, brown and fragrant, they made a supper or breakfast one could rejoice in.

Backbone stewed, and served with sweet potatoes, hot corn bread, and sparkling cider, was certainly not to be despised. The stewing was gentle, the seasoning well blended—enough salt but not too much, red and black pepper, and the merest dash of pepper vinegar. Many cooks left the vinegar to be added in the plates. There was little water at the beginning, and next to none at the end—the kettle was kept well covered, and not allowed to boil over. Backbone pie held its own with chicken pie—indeed there were those who preferred it. It was made the same way— in a skillet or deep pan lined with rich crust, then filled with cooked meat, adding strips of bacon, and bits of butter rolled in flour, as well as strips of crust. Then the stewing liquor went into the crevices —there might also be a few very tiny crisp brown sausages—cakes no bigger than a lady's watch. Over all came a thick, rich crust, with a cross-cut in the middle, and corners turned deftly back. When the crust was brown the pie was done.

No doubt we were foolish—but somehow the regular "cases" made our sausages unappetizing if we put it into them for keeping. Further the "Tom Thumbs" were in great request for chitterlings—I never saw them served to white folks but have smelled their savoriness in the cabins. That is, however, beside the mark. We saved our sausage against the spring scarcity in several ways. One was to fry it in quantity, pack the cakes as fried in crocks, pour over them the gravy, and when the jar was almost full, cover the top an inch deep with melted lard. Kept cool and dark the cakes came out as good as they went in. Still there were palates that craved smoked sausage. To satisfy them, some folk tied up the meat in links of clean corn husks, and hung them at the side where the smoke barely touched them. Another way was to make small bags of stout unbleached muslin, fill, tie close, dip the bag in melted grease, cool and smoke. The dipping was not really essential—still it kept the sausage a little fresher. Latterly I have been wondering if paraffin had been known then whether or not it would have served better than grease.

Hams and Other Hams

The proper boiling of a proper ham
reaches the level of high art. Proper boiling makes any sound ham tolerable eating; conversely a crass and hasty cook can
spoil utterly this crowning mercy of the
smokehouse. Yet proper cooking is not
a recondite process, nor one beyond the
simplest intelligence. It means first and
most, pains and patience, with somewhat
of foresight, and something more of judgment.

Cut off the hock, but not too high—barely
the slender shankbone. Then go all over
the ham with a dull knife, scraping off every bit of removable grease or soilure.

Wipe afterward with a coarse, damp cloth, then lay in a dishpan and cover an inch deep with cold water. If the water is very hard soften by adding a tiny pinch of baking soda. Leave in soak all night. In the morning wash well all over, using your coarse cloth, and a little scouring soap, then rinse well in tepid water, followed by a second rinsing in cold water, drain, and wipe dry. A flat-bottomed boiler is best —with one rounding, there is greater risk of scorching. Set a rack on the bottom else an old dish or earthen pieplate, pour in an inch of water, set over the fire, lay the ham upon the rack, skin side down, and fill up with cold water till it stands two inches above the meat. Take care in adding the water not to dislodge the ham from the rack. Bring the water to a boil, throw in a pint of cold water and skim the boiler very clean, going over it twice or three times. After the last skimming add half a dozen whole cloves, a dozen whole alspice, a pod of red pepper, a few whole grains of black pepper, and if you like, a young onion or a stalk of celery. Person-

ally I do not like either onion or celery—
moreover they taint the fat one may save
from the pot. Let the water boil hard for
half a minute, no longer, then slack heat till
it barely simmers. Keep it simmering, filling up the pot as the water in it boils
away, until the ham is tender throughout.
The time depends on several things—the
hardness and age of the ham, weight, curing. Fifteen minutes to the pound, reckoned from the beginning of simmering, is
the standard allowance. I have no hard
and fast rule—my hams boil always until
the fork pierces them readily, and the hip-
bone stands clear of flesh.

A big ham, fifteen to twenty pounds
weight, had better be left in the water
overnight. A smaller one, say of ten
pounds weight, should remain only until
thoroughly cold. Take up carefully when
cold, let drain twenty minutes, lying flesh
side up in a flat dish, then trim off the
under side and edges neatly, removing
rusty fat, strings, etc., and cutting through
the skin at the hock end. Turn over and
remove the skin—taking care not to tear

away too much fat with it. Remove the ham to a clean, deep dish, or bowl—the closer fitting the better, then pour around it either sound claret, or sweet cider, till it stands half way up the sides. Add a little tabasco or Worcester to the liquor, if high flavors are approved. Then stick whole cloves in a lozenge pattern all over the fat, sprinkle on thickly red and black pepper, and last of all, sugar—brown sugar if to be had, but white will do.

Leave standing several hours, basting once or twice with the liquor in the bowl. Take out, set on a rack in an agate pan, pour the liquor underneath, and bake slowly one to two hours, according to size. Baste every fifteen minutes, adding water as the liquor cooks away. Beware scorching—the ham should be a beautiful speckly dark brown all over. Let cool uncovered, and keep cool, but not on ice until eaten.

Drop a lump of ice in the boiling liquor unless the weather is cold—then set it outside. As soon as the fat on top hardens take it off, boil it fifteen minutes in clear water, chill, skim off, and clarify by frying slices of raw potato in it. The spices will have sunk to the bottom, and there will be no trace of their flavor in the fat. Any boiling vegetable—cabbage, string beans, navy beans, greens in general —may be cooked to advantage in the liquor. It also serves as an excellent foundation for pea soup. Drain it off from the sediment, reduce a trifle by quick boiling, then add the other things. Dumplings of sound cornmeal, wet up stiff, shaped the size of an egg, and dropped in the boiling liquor, furnish a luncheon dish cheap and appetizing.

Fried ham as Mammy made it is mostly a fragrant memory—only plutocrats dare indulge in it these days. She cut thin slices from the juicy, thick part of the ham, using a very sharp, clean knife. Then she trimmed away the skin, and laid the slices in a clean, hot skillet—but not too hot. In about a minute she flipped them over delicately, so as to sear the other side. When enough fat had been tried out to bubble a bit, she turned them again, then set the skillet off, deadened the coals beneath it a little—put it back, and let the ham cook until tender through and through. She never washed the slices nor even wiped them with damp cloths. There was no need—her hands and knife were as clean as could be. Washing and wiping spoiled the flavor, she said. I agree with her. After the ham was taken up, she poured in milk, half cream, shook it well about in the hissing hot fat until it had taken up all the delicious brown essence caked on the skillet bottom. This milk gravy was poured over the slices in the platter. A practice I have never followed—my gravy is made with water rather than milk, and served separately.

Invalids and gourmets may be indulged with boiled ham, broiled over live coals. Slice very thin, lay for half a minute upon a shovel of glowing fresh coals, take up in a very hot dish, butter liberally, dust with pepper and serve very hot. To frizzle ham slice as thin as possible in tiny bits, and toss the bits till curly-crisp in blazing hot butter. Excellent as an appetizer or to raise a thirst.

For ham and eggs slice and fry as directed, take up, break fresh eggs separately each in a saucer, and slip them into the fat when it is bubbling hot. Dip hot fat over them to cook the upper side—take up with a cake turner, and arrange prettily as a border around the ham. Sprigs of watercress outside add to the appetizing effect. Serve with hot biscuit, or waffles or muffins, and strong, clear coffee.

Tart apples cored but not peeled sliced in rings and fried in hot fat, drained out and sprinkled lightly with sugar, add to the charm of even the finest ham. So does hominy, the full-grained sort, boiled tender beforehand, and fried till there is a thick, brown crust all over the skillet bottom. The secret of these as of all other fryings, is to have grease enough, make it hot enough to crisp whatever goes into it instantly, then to watch so there shall be no scorching, and take out what is fried as soon as done, draining well. Among the paradoxes of cookery is this —frying with scant grease makes greasy eating, whereas frying in deep fat, sufficiently hot, makes the reverse.

Sweet potatoes, peeled and sliced, deserve frying in ham fat. Well drained, dusted with salt, pepper, and sugar, they are delicious, also most digestible. Frying is indeed the method of cookery most misprised through its abuse. In capable hands it achieves results no-otherwise attainable.

A perfect mutton ham is a matter of grace no less premeditation. It must be cut from a wether at least four years old, grass fed, grain finished, neither too fat, nor too lean, scientifically butchered in clear, frosty, but not freezing weather, and hung unsalted in clean, cold air for a matter of three days. Saw off shank and hip bones neatly, and cut the meat smooth, removing any tags and jags, then pack down in an agate or clean wooden vessel that has been scalded, then chilled. Half cover with a marinade thus proportioned. One pint pickling salt to one gallon cold water, boil and skim clean, then add one pint vinegar, a dozen each of whole cloves,

allspice and pepper corns, a pod of red
pepper, a teaspoon of powdered saltpeter,
and a small cup of oil. Simmer for half
an hour, and cool before pouring on the
meat. Let it lie in the liquor a week, turning it twice daily. Take from marinade,
wipe, and lay in air, return the marinade
to the fire, boil up, skim well, then add
enough plain brine to fully cover the hams,
skim again, cool and pour over, first scalding out the containing vessel. Let stand
a week longer, then drain well, wipe with
a damp cloth, rub over outside with a mixture of salt, moist sugar, and ground black
pepper, and hang in a cool, airy place
where the hams can be lightly smoked for
a fortnight. Winter-curing, or late fall,
alone is possible to the average house-
holder. After smoking, wrap in waxed
paper, and canvas the same as other hams.

Cook the same as venison, which mutton thus cured much resembles. Slice and
broil, serving with butter and very sour
jelly, else boil whole in very little water until tender, glazing with tart jelly, and crisp-
ing in the oven after draining and cooling.

Or soak two hours in cold water, then cover completely with an inch-thick crust of flour and water mixed stiff, and bake in a slow oven four to five hours. Serve always with very piquant sauce, and sharp pickle, or highly spiced catsups. Make jelly from wild grapes, wild plums, green grapes, green gooseberries or crab apples, using half the usual amount of sugar, especially for such meat.

Melt half a glass of such jelly with a tablespoon of boiling water. Add black pepper, paprika, a dash of tabasco, and the strained juice of a lemon, add gradually a teaspoon of dry mustard. Cook over hot water until well mixed and smooth, and keep hot until served.

Beef hams are troublesome—but worth the trouble. Take them from small but well fatted animals, cut off the shank, also part of the top round. Rub over very scantly with powdered saltpeter, mixed well through moist sugar, then lay down in salt for a fortnight, else cover with brine made thus. Pint pickling salt to the gallon of cold water, teaspoon sugar, and pinch of whole cloves. Boil and skim. Pour cold over the hams in a clean barrel. Let stand a fortnight, take out, drain and wipe, rub over with dry salt, and hang high in cold air. Smoke lightly after three days. Keep smoking, but not too much, for a month. Cover all over with ground black pepper, mixed to a paste with molasses, canvas and leave hanging.

Slice and broil, else chip and serve raw. Frizzling is possible but a waste of God's good mercies. Properly cured meat is salt but not too salt, of a deep blackish-red, and when sliced thin, partly translucent, also of an indescribable savoriness. Cut as nearly as possible, across the grain. Do not undertake to make beef hams save in the late fall, so there may be cold weather for the curing. The meat must be chilled through before salt touches it, but freezing is very detrimental. Frozen meat does not absorb the salt, sugar, etc., essential to proper curing. By time it thaws so absorption becomes possible, there may have been changes such as take place in cold storage, unfitting it for food.

If the beef ham is thick it may need to lie a month in salt or in brine. Here as elsewhere, the element of judgment comes into play.

If rabbits are very plenty and very fat, put down a jar of hindquarters in marinade for three days, then wipe, and hang in a cold, dry place. A rabbit ought to be dressed before it is cold—thus it escapes the strong flavor which makes market rabbits often unendurable. Chill but do not freeze after dressing. A light smoking does not hurt the quarters, which should be left double, with the thick loin between. Soak two hours before cooking, and smother with plenty of butter, black and red pepper and a dash of pepper vinegar. An excellent breakfast or luncheon relish.

To cook a fresh ham properly, choose one weighing ten pounds or less, scrape and wash clean, score the skin, all over, then season well with salt, sugar, black and red pepper, and dot with tabasco on top. Set on a rack in a deep pan, pour boiling water underneath to barely touch the meat, cover close, and bake in a hot oven for two hours, filling up the water in the pan as it bakes away. Uncover, and cook for half an hour longer, slacking heat one half, and basting the meat with the liquor in the pan. If approved add a cup of cider or sound claret to the basting liquor. Leave unbasted for ten minutes before taking up, so the skin may be properly crisp.

For Thirsty Souls

Grandmother's Cherry Bounce: Rinse a clean, empty whiskey barrel well with cold water, drain, and fill with very ripe Morello cherries, mixed with black wild cherries. One gallon wild cherries to five of Morellos is about the proper proportion. Strew scantly through the cherries, blade mace, whole cloves, allspice, a very little bruised ginger, and grated nutmeg. Add to a full barrel of fruit twenty pounds of sugar—or in the proportion of half a pound to the gallon of fruit. Cover the fruit an inch deep with good corn whiskey, the older and milder the better. Leave out the bung but cover the opening with lawn. Let stand six months undisturbed in a dry, airy place, rather warm. Rack off into a clean barrel, let stand six months longer, then bottle or put in demijohns. This improves greatly with age up to the fifth year—after that the change is unappreciable.

Grape Cider: Fill a clean, tight, well-scalded barrel with ripe wild grapes picked from their stems. Add spices if you like, but they can be left out. Fill the vessel with new cider, the sweeter the better. There should be room left to ferment. Cover the bung-hole with thin cloth and let stand in dry air four to six months. Rack off and bottle. This also improves with age. It is a drink to be used with caution—mild as May in the mouth, but heady, and overcoming, especially to those unused to its seductions.

Persimmon Beer: The poor relation of champagne—with the advantage that nobody is ever the worse for drinking it. To make it, take full-ripe persimmons, the juicier the better, free them of stalks and calyxes, then mash thoroughly, and add

enough wheat bran or middlings to make
a stiffish dough. Form the dough into
thin, flat cakes, which bake crisp in a slow
oven. When cold break them up in a clean
barrel, and fill it with filtered rainwater.
A bushel of persimmons before mashing
will make a barrel of beer. Set the barrel
upright, covered with a thin cloth, in a
warm, dry place, free of taints. Let stand
until the beer works—the persimmon cakes
will rise and stand in a foamy mass on top.
After three to four weeks, either move the
barrel to a cold place, or rack off the beer
into bottles or demijohns, tieing down the
corks, and keeping the bottled stuff very
cool. The more meaty and flavorous the
persimmons, the richer will be the beer.
Beware of putting in fruit that has not
felt the touch of frost, so retains a rough
tang. A very little of it will spoil a whole
brewing of beer. If the beer is left standing in the barrel a wooden cover should be
laid over the cloth, after it is done working. Fermentation can be hastened by
putting in with the persimmon cakes a
slice of toast dipped in quick yeast. But

if the temperature is right, the beer will ferment itself.

Egg Nogg: Have all ingredients, eggs, sugar, brandy, and whiskey, thoroughly chilled before beginning, and work very, very quickly. Beat the yolks of eighteen eggs very light with six cups of granulated sugar, added a cup at a time. When frothy and pale yellow, beat in gradually and alternately a glassful at a time, a quart of mellow old whiskey, and a quart of real French brandy. Whip hard, then add the whites of the eggs beaten till they stick to the dish. Grate nutmeg over the top, and rub the rims of the serving glasses with lemon or orange rind cut into the fruit. The glasses should be ice-cold, also the spoons. Fill carefully so as not to slop the sides, and serve at once.

If wanted for an early morning Christmas celebration, beat up yolks and sugar the night before, stand on ice along with the liquor, and keep the unbeaten whites likewise very cold. At morning freshen the yolks a little, then add the liquor, and at last the whites newly frothed. This is

the only simon-pure Christmas egg nogg.
Those who put into it milk, cream, what
not, especially rum, defile one of the finest
among Christmas delights.

White Egg Nogg: For invalids, especially fever patients. Whip the white of
a new laid egg as stiff as possible with the
least suspicion of salt. Add to it three
heaping spoonfuls of sterilized cream
whipped light, beat in two tablespoonfuls
of powdered sugar, then add a gill of the
best French brandy. A variant is to omit
the sugar and mix with the frothed egg
and cream more than a gill of vermouth,
using French or Italian, according to
taste.

Apple Toddy: Wash and core, but do
not peel, six large, fair apples, bake, covered, until tender through and through,
put into an earthen bowl and strew with
cloves, mace, and bruised ginger, also six
lumps of Domino sugar for each apple.
Pour over a quart of full-boiling water, let
stand covered fifteen minutes in a warm
place. Then add a quart of mellow whiskey, leave standing ten minutes longer,

and keep warm. Serve in big deep goblets, putting an apple or half of one in the bottom of each, and filling with the liquor. Grate nutmeg on top just at the minute of serving.

Hail Storm: Mix equal quantities of clear ice, broken small, and the best lump sugar. Cover the mixture fully with good brandy, put in a shaker, shake hard five minutes, then pour into glasses, and serve with a fresh mint leaf floating on top.

Mint Julep: This requires the best of everything if you would have it in perfection. Especially the mint and the whiskey or brandy. Choose tender, quick-grown mint, leafy, not long-stalked and coarse, wash it very clean, taking care not to bruise it in the least, and lay in a clean cloth upon ice. Chill the spirits likewise. Put the sugar and water in a clean fruit jar, and set on ice. Do this at least six hours before serving so the sugar shall be fully dissolved. Four lumps to the large goblet is about right—with half a gobletful of fresh cold water. At serving time, rub a zest of lemon around the rim of each

goblet—the goblets must be well chilled—
then half fill with the dissolved sugar, add
a tablespoonful of cracked ice, and stand
sprigs of mint thickly all around the rim.
Set the goblets in the tray, then fill up with
whiskey or brandy or both, mixed—the
mixture is best with brands that blend
smoothly. Drop in the middle a fresh ripe
strawberry, or cherry, or slice of red peach,
and serve at once. Fruit can be left out
without harm to flavor—it is mainly for the
satisfaction of the eye. But never by any
chance bruise the mint—it will give an
acrid flavor "most tolerable and not to be
endured." To get the real old-time effect,
serve with spoons in the goblets rather than
straws. In dipping and sipping more of
the mint-essence comes out—beside the
clinking of the spoons is nearly as refreshing as the tinkle of the ice.

Lemon Punch: Bring a gallon of fresh
water to a bubbling boil in a wide kettle,
and as it strikes full boil throw into it a
tablespoonful of tea—whatever brand you
like best. Let boil one minute—no more,
no less, then strain, boiling hot, upon the

juice and thin yellow peel of twelve large or eighteen small lemons, along with two pounds of lump sugar. Stir hard until the sugar is dissolved, then add a pint of rum. Stand on ice twelve to twenty-four hours to blend and ripen. Put a small block of clear ice in the punch bowl, pour in the punch, then add to it either Maraschino cherries, or hulled small ripe strawberries, or pineapple or bananas, peeled and cut in tiny dice—or a mixture of all these. Serve in chilled punch cups, with after-dinner coffee spoons for the fruit. The fruit can be left out, and the punch served with sandwiches the same as iced tea. A wineglass of yellow chartreuse, added just after the rum, is to many palates an improvement. So is a very little peach or apricot brandy.

Punch à la Ruffle Shirts: This recipe comes down from the epoch of knee buckles and ruffled shirts, and is warranted to more than hold its own with any other—even the so-famous "Artillery punch," beloved of army and navy. To make it, scrub clean and pare thinly the yellow peel of two

dozen oranges and one dozen lemons. Put
the pared peel in a deep glass pitcher and
cover it with one quart of brandy, one quart
of old whiskey, one generous pint of Ja-
maica rum, one tumbler of cherry bounce,
one tumbler of peach liqueur, or else a tumbler of "peach and honey." Cover with
cloth and let stand three days off ice to
blend and ripen. Meantime squeeze and
strain the juice of the oranges and lemons
upon four pounds of best lump sugar, shred
a large, very ripe pineapple fine and put it
with another pound of sugar in a separate
vessel. Hull half a gallon of ripe strawberries, cover them liberally with sugar
and let stand to extract the juice. Lacking strawberries, use ripe peaches, or
blackberries or even seeded cherries.
Keep the fruit and sugar cool, but not too
cold—just so it will not sour. Upon the
third morning strain the juice of all fruits
together, and mix thoroughly. Next make
a gallon of weak green tea, strain it boiling hot upon the liquor and the yellow peel,
stir well, then mix in the fruit juices and
sugar, and let stand uncovered until cool.

Chill thoroughly, also chill the wine. Use whatever sort you prefer—claret, sound and fruity, is good, so is almost any home-made wine of the first class. American champagne pleases some palates. But I advise rather claret, or good homemade grape wine. Put into the punch bowl a block of clear ice, add equal measures of the mixture and the wine. Let stand half an hour before serving. Put in at the very last vichy, ice-cold. Thin strips of fresh cucumber peel add a trifle to flavor and more to looks.

The wine and mixture can be poured together into demijohns and kept for months, provided they are kept cool. Since the making is rather troublesome it is worth while to make the full quantity at once and keep it on hand for emergencies. Commercial liqueurs can take the place of the homemade ones here set forth. The result may not be quite so distinctive, but will not be disappointing. Dry sherry is a good substitute for cherry bounce, likewise apricot brandy, while vermouth or chartreuse will answer for peach liqueur, which is unlikely to be in hand unless you are a very old-fashioned housekeeper.

Peach Liqueur: Peel a peck of very ripe, very juicy peaches, cut from the seed, weigh, and pack down in earthen or agate ware with their own weight in granulated sugar. Crack the seeds, take out the kernels, blanche the same as almonds, and put to soak in a quart of brandy. Let stand in sunshine to extract the flavor, a full day. Let the fruit and sugar stand twenty-four hours, then put over fire in a preserving kettle and simmer very slowly until the fruit is in rags, adding now and then enough boiling water to make up for what cooks out. If spices are approved, simmer with the fruit, a pinch of blade mace, some whole cloves and half a dozen black pepper corns. This is optional. Strain without pressing to avoid cloudiness, and mix the juice while still very hot with the brandy and soaked kernels. Add brandy and kernels, also a quart of whiskey—there should be a gallon of the fruit juice. Stir hard so as to blend well. Let cool, and bottle or put in demijohns, taking care to apportion the kernels equally. They will sink to the bottom, but the liqueur will fatten on them, getting thereby a delicate almond fragrance and flavor.

Strawberry Liqueur: Wash, hull and mash two gallons of very ripe strawberries, put over the fire, bring to a quick boil, skim clean, and simmer for five minutes. Throw in a pint of boiling water, and strain as for jelly. Measure the juice—for each pint take a pound of sugar, return to the kettle, simmer fifteen minutes, skimming clean the while, then take from the fire, measure, and to each quart add a pint of good whiskey, or whiskey and brandy mixed. Bottle while still hot, and seal. Small bottles are best. By adding spices to taste while the juice is simmering you turn the liqueur into strawberry cordial.

Blackberry Cordial: Pick over, wash and drain well half a bushel of very ripe, but sound berries. Mash, add a very little cold water, and simmer for half an hour, then strain and measure the juice. Put a pound of sugar to each pint, and to each gallon, a teaspoon of cloves, the same of allspice, a race of ginger well bruised, a tiny pod of Cayenne pepper, and a half dozen black pepper corns. Tie the spices loosely in very thin muslin so they may not be skimmed off. Skim away all froth, and cook for an hour, keeping the kettle barely boiling. It should reduce about one-half. Take from the fire and add spirits, either whiskey or brandy, in the proportion of one to two—two pints cordial to one of liquor. Let cool uncovered, bottle and cork tight—sealing is unnecessary. Excellent for convalescents, especially children. To make it almost a specific for bowel troubles, dig up, and wash clean, dewberry roots, cut short, and boil in clear water, making a very strong decoction. Add this to the cordial while still boiling, in proportion of one to four. Then mix in the spirits. A quart of cordial can be thus treated medicinally, and the rest kept for ordinary uses.

Blackberry Wine: Pick, wash, and mash thoroughly, sound ripe berries, pour upon each gallon a gallon of freshly-boiling water, and let stand twenty-four hours.

Strain, measure juice, allow three and one-half pounds sugar to each gallon of it. Put into clean cask or jugs, do not fill, but leave room for fermentation. Cover mouth or bung-hole with thin cloth, and let stand in clean warm air for two months. Rack off into clean vessels, throwing away the lees, and cork or cover close. Fit for use in another month. Improves with age up to a year.

Strawberry Wine: Mash thoroughly clean, hulled, very ripe berries, add equal bulk of boiling water, let stand six hours, then strain. Put the strained juice in a preserving kettle with two and a half pounds of sugar to each gallon. Bring to a boil, skim clean, then pour into clean vessels, close mouths with thin cloth, and let stand until fermentation ceases. In a wet season the berries are likely to be so juicy, less water is required—or more sugar necessary.

Gooseberry Wine: Wash and drain dead-ripe gooseberries, mash them thoroughly with a wooden pestle, and add their own bulk of boiling water. Let stand thirty-six hours unless the weather is very warm—then twenty-four will be long enough. Press out all the juice, even though it runs muddy. Measure, and to each gallon add three pounds down-weight, of the best lump sugar. Stir well, repeating every day for a week, then cover with lawn and let stand till fermentation ceases. Cover tight then and leave standing six weeks longer, so the wine may fatten on the lees. Rack off carefully, filtering the muddy part at the bottom through several thicknesses of cheese cloth. Put in a clean vessel for two months longer, then bottle and seal. If the bottles are laid on the side, and the wine carefully decanted it will show a bright golden yellow with much the translucence of topaz. It reaches perfection at a year. Being rather heavy it is improved to many palates by adding ice-cold vichy after it is in the glasses.

Grape Wine: Pick from stems, wash, drain, and mash thoroughly, ripe sound grapes. Add measure for measure of full-boiling water, and let stand twelve hours. If very deep color is desired, and the grapes are black, let stand twenty-four. Strain, measure juice, add to each gallon three pounds of sugar, stir till dissolved, then put in a clean vessel, filling it only three-parts, cover the mouth with lawn, and let stand in clean warm air until fermentation ceases. Close tight then, and let stand a month longer, then rack off, filter last runnings through triple cheese cloth, bottle and cork tight. Keep where it is dark and warm, rather than cool, but away from any sort of taints.

Muscadine Wine: Troublesome, but worth the trouble. Wash dead-ripe muscadines, and pop them one by one, out of the skins. Throw away the skins, after squeezing all juice from them—if the pulp stood with them their burning, musky taste would ruin it. Cover it with half its bulk of boiling water. Let stand a day and night, then strain, and add to each gallon of juice three pounds of white rock-candy. Stir every day until the candy dissolves. Cover with cloth until it is through fermenting. Rack off, bottle immediately, and seal, or tie down the corks. The wine in perfection is a pale pink, very clear, and of a peculiar but indescribably delicious flavor.

Fruit Vinegars: Any sort of acid fruit —as strawberries, raspberries, gooseberries, currants, black or red, affords a refreshing drink.   Pick, wash, put over the fire to scald—when it has boiled a minute or two add half as much cold water as fruit, and bring again to a boil.   Skim clean, take from fire and let stand till next day.   Strain, then measure juice, add two to three pounds sugar to the gallon, according to tartness desired, put over the fire, and simmer for twenty minutes, skimming clean.   Boil in it spices most liked, tied up in thin muslin.   If it seems watery, boil another twenty minutes till the syrup shows rather rich, then add, after taking from the fire, a quart of cider vinegar for each gallon of syrup, mix well, bottle while still hot in small bottles, cork and seal. Mixed half and half with ice water, or poured over finely broken ice, or as a flavoring to tea, hot or cold, this is refreshing, particularly in hot weather. Use in tea a spoonful to the cup or glass.

Boiled Cider: Reduce new sweet cider one-half by gentle boiling, skimming it clean as it boils, then bottle, putting a clove or two, a grain of alspice and a blade of mace in each bottle. Cork, seal and keep in a cool place. This is especially valuable for use in mincemeat, or for flavoring sauces for nursery puddings. A variant is to add sugar towards the last, enough to make a thinnish syrup, which is of itself a good sauce for simple desserts.

Paste, Pies, Puddings

The Philosophy of Pie Crust: Pie-crust perfection depends on several things —good flour, good fat, good handling, most especially good baking. A hot oven, quick but not scorching, expands the air betwixt layers of paste, and pops open the flour-grains, making them absorb the fat as it melts, thereby growing crisp and relishful instead of hard and tough. The lighter and drier the flour the better—in very damp weather it is best oven-dried, then cooled before mixing. Shortening, whether lard, butter, or clarified drippings, should be very cold—unless your recipe demands that it be softened or melted. Milk or water used in mixing ought to be likewise well chilled, unless the shortening is soft —in that case match its temperature. The regular rule is half-pint ice water to the pound of flour, using chilled shortening. If the fat is semi-fluid the paste must be mixed softer, using say, three parts of a pint to the pound.

Baking powder or soda and cream tartar, or soda alone with sour cream or buttermilk for wetting, makes crust light and short with less butter, therefore is an economy. Genuine puff paste is requisite for the finest tarts, pies, etc., etc., but light short crust answers admirably for most things. Sift flour twice or even thrice for any sort of paste. Sift soda or baking powder well through it, but not salt. Make the salt fine, drop in the bottom of the mixing bowl, before the last sifting, and mix lightly through the flour before adding the shortening. Rub in shortening very lightly, using only the finger-tips— the palms melt or soften it. Add milk or water, a little at a time, mixing it in with a broad-bladed knife rather than the hands. Mix lightly—so the paste barely sticks together. Put in first one-third of the shortening—this, of course, for puff paste. Half a pound of butter or lard to the pound of flour makes a very good paste, but to have it in full richness, use three-quarters of a pound. Wash butter well to remove the salt, and squeeze out water by wringing it in a well-floured cloth. If there is a strong taste, or any trace of rancidity, wash well, kneading through and through, in sweet milk, then rinse out the milk with cold water to which a little borax has been added. Rinse again in clear cold water—this should remove ill-flavor without injury to anybody's stomach. But be very sure the last rinsing is thorough—borax, though wholly harmless, adds nothing to digestibility.

The end of the repeated rollings out and foldings demanded by real puff paste is to enclose between the layers of paste as much air as possible. Hence the chillings between rollings. Hence also the need of pinching edges well together after foldings, and rolling always *from* you, never back and forth. Roll out paste into a long narrow strip after the first mixing, divide the remaining shortening into three equal portions, keep very cold, and as needed cut into small bits, which spread evenly on top of the rolled paste, which must be lightly dredged with flour. Fold in three evenly, one thickness on another, turn so the folded edges may be to right and left while rolling, pinch the other edges well together and roll again into a long strip, moving the rolling-pin always from you. Repeat until all the butter is used, then set on ice for an hour to harden. In baking beware opening the oven door until the paste has risen fully and becomes slightly crusted over.

Baking powder crust must not stand— the gas which aerates it begins forming and escaping the minute it is wet up. It also requires a hot oven and delicate handling. Half a pound of shortening and a teaspoon of baking powder, to the pound of flour, mixed stiff or soft, according to the consistency of the fat, properly handled and baked, make crust good enough for anybody.

French Puff Paste: This is like the famous little girl—either very good indeed or horrid. Therefore beware undertaking it until you have experience or the confidence of absolute ignorance for your help. Either may take you on to success—when half-knowledge or half-confidence will spell disaster. You need for it, two pounds, thrice sifted flour, two pounds well-washed and very cold butter, four egg-yolks well chilled, and half a pint, more or less, of ice water, also a saltspoon of fine salt. Rub four ounces of butter lightly into the flour, shape the rest into a flattish oblong and set on ice. Wet the flour with the egg-yolks and water, adding them alternately, work smooth, handling as lightly as possible, then roll out half an inch thick, dredge lightly with flour, lay on the ball of cold butter, fold paste over it smoothly, flatten lightly with strokes of the rolling-pin, then roll out as thin as possible without making the butter break through.

Fold again in three, roll again, as thin as you can. Repeat folding and rolling, then set on ice half an hour, folding in three. Roll and fold twice again, chill again for twenty minutes, then give two more rolls and foldings. Chill if possible before using. If all things have worked well you will have crust that is an experience.

Every Day Pie Crust: One pound flour, six ounces shortening—lard or clarified dripping, pinch salt, half-pint ice water. Mix flour, salt and water to a smooth dough, using a broad knife, roll out thin, spread with a third of the fat, fold in three, roll out again, add another third of fat, roll, add the last fat, roll again, fold and chill for ten minutes before using.

Cobblers: Make from any sort of fruit in season—peaches, apples, cherries, plums or berries. Green gooseberries are inadvisable, through being too tart and too tedious. Stone cherries, pare peaches or apples and slice thin, halve plums if big enough, and remove stones—if not, wash, drain well, and use whole. Line a skillet or deep pie pan—it must be three inches deep at least, liberally with short crust, rolled rather more than a quarter-inch thick. Fit well, then prick all over with a blunt fork. Fill with the prepared fruit, put on an upper crust a quarter-inch thick and plenty big enough, barely press the crust edges together, prick well with a fork all over the top, and cook in a hot oven half to three-quarters of an hour, according to size. Take up, remove top crust, lay it inverted upon another plate, sweeten the hot fruit liberally, adding if you like, a spoonful of brandy, adding also a good lump of the best butter. Mix well through the fruit, then dip out enough of it to make a thick layer over the top crust. Grate nutmeg over apple pies, or strew on a little powdered cinnamon. A few blades of mace baked with the fruit accent the apple flavor beautifully. Cherries take kindly to brandy, but require less butter than either peaches or apples. Give plums plenty of sugar with something over for the stones. Cook a few stones with them for flavor, even if you take away the bulk.

Do the same with cherries, using, say, a dozen pits to the pie.

Serve cobbler hot or cold. If hot, serve with it hard brandy sauce, made by creaming together a cup of sugar, a tablespoonful of butter, then working in two tablespoonfuls of brandy or good whiskey. Right here is perhaps the place to say once for all, good whiskey is far and away better in anything than poor brandy. Thick sweet cream whipped or plain, sets off cold cobbler wonderfully to the average palate.

Fried Pies: To be perfect these must be made of sun-dried peaches, very bright and sweet, but any sort of sound dried fruit will serve at a pinch. Soak overnight after washing in three waters, simmer five hours in the soaking water, with a plate to hold the fruit under, mash and sweeten while hot, adding spices to taste—cinnamon, nutmeg and grated lemon peel for apples, cloves and ginger—a bare zest— for peaches or apricots. Roll out short paste into rounds the size of a small plate, cover one-half with the fruit, fold over the empty half, pinch well together around the edges, and fry in deep fat, blazing hot, to a rich quick brown on both sides. Drain on paper napkins, sprinkling lightly with sugar. Serve hot or cold. Most excellent for impromptu luncheons or very late suppers—withal wholesome. A famous doctor said often of them, "You would be only the better for eating an acre of them."

Green Apple Pie: Take apples a little bigger than the thumb's end, cut off stalks and nibs, and slice crosswise in three, dropping them in water as sliced to save discoloration. Make a rich syrup—three cups sugar, one cup water, to four cups sliced fruit. Boil and skim, throw in the apples, with a blade or so of mace, and cook quickly until preserved through. Either bake between crust in the common way, or bake crust crisp after pricking well, and spread with the preserved fruit. Else make into small turnovers, but bake instead of frying them—and be sure the oven is hot enough to brown, but not to burn. Or you may make the green apples into shortcake, putting fruit only between the layers of crust, and serving with rich sauce or sweetened cream.

Lemon Custard: (M. L. Williams.) Separate and beat very light, the yolks and whites of six eggs. Beat into the yolks very smoothly one pound of sugar, then half a pound of creamed butter. Mix well, then add the beaten whites, followed by the strained juice and grated yellow peel of two large or three small lemons. Beat five minutes longer, pour into pans lined with puff paste, pop into a hot oven and bake to a bright brown. Meringue can be added but is not necessary save for ornament.

Cream Pie: (M. L. Williams.) Beat three eggs very light with a heaping cup of sugar, add two cups sifted flour, mix smooth, then put in half a cup of rich sour cream with half-teaspoon soda dissolved in it. Mix, put instantly into shallow pans, bake in a quick oven and serve hot with or without sauce.

Damson and Banana Tart: (M. W. Watkins.) An heirloom in the relator's family, coming down from English fore-

bears.   Line an agate or earthen pie dish
two to three inches deep, with very good
crust, rolled thin, but not stretched nor
dragged. Cover it with bananas, sliced
thin, lengthwise, strew over three tablespoonfuls of sugar, and a pinch of grated
lemon peel. Sprinkle with a liqueur glass
of rum or brandy or whiskey, then put in
a layer of preserved plums—damsons are
best—along with their juice. If there is
room repeat the layers—bananas and
plums and seasoning. Cover with a crust
rolled fairly thin, prick and bake three-
quarters of an hour in a moderately quick
oven. Serve either hot or cold, preferably
hot, with this sauce. One egg beaten very
light, with a cupful of cream, a wineglass
of rum, brandy or sherry, and a larger
glass of preserve syrup. Mix over hot
water, stirring hard all the time till it
begins to thicken. It must not get too
thick.

Amber Pie: (Mrs. J. R. Oldham.) Beat
yolks of four eggs very light, with two
heaping cups sugar, large spoonful melted
butter, rounding teaspoon sifted flour, cup

buttermilk, cup seeded raisins, teaspoon cinnamon, pinch each of cloves, alspice and nutmeg, two whites of egg beaten very stiff. Half bake crust, then pour in batter and cook slowly until done. Cover with meringue made by beating two egg-whites with two teaspoons cold water, a few grains of salt, and one cup sugar. Add sugar gradually after eggs are very light. Use at once—it will fall by standing. Let the meringue barely color in the oven. Serve hot or cold.

Jelly Pie: (Louise Williams.) Beat the yolks of four eggs very light, with a cup of sugar, three-quarters cup creamed butter, and a glass of jelly, the tarter the better. Add a tablespoonful vanilla and a dessert-spoonful of sifted cornmeal, then the whites of eggs beaten very stiff. Bake in crusts—this makes two fat pies. Meringue is optional—and unnecessary.

Cheese Cakes: Beat until very light the yolks of twelve eggs with a pound of sugar, add to them a tablespoonful cornstarch, then three-quarters of a pound of butter, washed and creamed. Add also the

strained juice of two lemons, a teaspoonful lemon essence and a teaspoonful vanilla. Set over boiling water and stir until
all ingredients blend—only thus can you
dissolve granulated sugar, which is best
to use, lacking the old-fashioned live open-
kettle brown. Keep over the hot water,
stirring well together as you fill the tart
shells. They must be lined with real puff
paste, rolled very thin, and nicely fitted.
Set in broad shallow pans, after filling
with the batter and bake in a quick, but
not scorching oven. A blanched almond,
or bit of citron, or half a pecan or walnut
meat, may be put in each shell before filling. I prefer though to add such frills
by help of the frosting. To make it, beat
six egg-whites with a pinch of salt until
they stick to the dish, add to them a little
at a time, three cups granulated sugar
boiled with a cup and a half of water, till
it spins a thread. Keep the syrup boiling
while adding it. When it is all in, set the
pan of frosting over boiling water, add six
drops lemon juice and beat until stiff
enough to hold shape. It must not touch

the water, but have plenty of steam rising underneath. Frost the tarts rather thickly, and stick either a shred of citron, a quarter of Maraschino cherry, or half a nut in the middle. If you like cocoanut flavor, strew freshly grated cocoanut over while the frosting is soft—it ought to harden inside half an hour. Tiny pink or green comfits stuck in the middle, or set in threes triangularly, are very decorative. Indeed, there is no limit but taste and invention to the manners of making beautiful these tarts. I rather pride myself upon them, since they have been enthusiastically praised by folk who have eaten all around the world, and set above the best of French confections by a man ten years resident in Paris, whose wife is held to be the most skilled amateur cook in New York.

Grated cocoanut or raw grated apple stirred into the batter before baking, varies the cheese cakes—and to some palates improves it. I myself find nothing quite to equal the cheese cake of my childhood— which had a full pound of butter to the pound of sugar, and no frills of frosting, though strips of citron were often latticed over the pans after the crust was in. Prick crust always very well before filling —thus the tarts will be shapely instead of caricatures.

Sweet Potato Custard: Boil tender two large or four medium sweet potatoes, peel, free of strings, and mash fine. Add to the pulp half a pound of creamed butter, mix well, then add gradually five cups sugar, alternately with five whole eggs. Beat smooth, add the juice of three lemons, a tablespoonful lemon essence, and a scant pint of very rich milk. Use less milk if the potatoes are very soft. Beat smooth and pour into pie pans lined with good crust. Bake brown in a quick oven, but do not over-bake. Lest the proportion of sugar may seem excessive, let it be said here that sweet potatoes require more sugar for sweetening than anything save crabapples or green gooseberries.

Sweet Potato Pie: Line a deep pie pan with short crust rolled a quarter-inch thick, fill it with raw sweet potatoes, peeled and sliced thin. Add to them, for a pan of medium size, three cups sugar, a cup of butter, cut in bits, mace, cloves and nutmeg to taste, half a cup cold water and half a cup good whiskey or sherry. Cover with a crust an eighth-inch thick, prick well, also cut a tiny cross in middle, and bake in a hot, but not scorching oven, three-quarters of an hour—a full hour if the pan is large. Turning another pan, fitting the rim over, helps to make the baking sure and even. Remove the cover pan ten minutes before taking up. Serve hot. This requires no sauce.

Apple Custard: Beat four eggs very light with three cups sugar, one cup butter, cup and a half rich milk—the richer the better. Stir in at the very last, one quart grated apple, flavor with nutmeg or vanilla, and bake in crusts. If wanted richer, dot raisins seeded and soaked in whiskey, or shred citron over the top before baking.

Molasses Pie: (M. W. Watkins.) Cream well together one large cup granulated sugar, and one heaping tablespoonful of butter, add when very light the well-beaten yolks of three eggs, and a large

cup of rich molasses. Flavor with one
teaspoonful grated nutmeg, then beat in,
at the very last, the whites of the eggs
frothed as stiff as possible. Bake in pans
lined with rich crust until firm. Meringue
can be added, but the pies do not need it.

Mystery Pie: (Louise Williams.) Beat
separately very light, the yolks and whites
of four eggs. Beat with the yolks a cup
and a half of sugar, three heaping tablespoonfuls of butter, two teaspoonfuls
mixed spices, either beaten or powdered
fine, one cup of tart dark jelly, one cup
blackberry jam, and one cup sweet milk.
Add last of all the egg-whites, mix in well,
then pour in pans lined with rich paste,
and bake until firm.

Butter Scotch Pie: (Leslie Fox.) Beat
light two egg-yolks with one scant cup
dark brown sugar, one tablespoonful
creamed butter, and two tablespoonfuls
flour. Mix smooth, then add gradually
one cup rich milk, put in double boiler, and
cook until thick. Let cool, flavor with vanilla, then pour into rich crusts, previously
well-baked, cover with meringue made

from the egg-whites, set in oven to harden, and serve hot or cold.

Raspberry Cream Pie: (Leslie Fox.) Line a deepish pie pan with very rich crust, spread the crust thickly with red raspberry jam, then pour upon it raw, a custard made from two eggs beaten well with one cup of milk, and one tablespoonful sugar. Bake until custard is well set, let cool, and spread with whipped cream. Serve cold as possible.

Rhubarb Pie: To a generous quart of rhubarb, peeled and cut up, put three cups sugar, the pulp scooped from three sweet oranges, thin bits of the yellow peel, two blades of mace broken small, and a scant half-cup of cold water. Cover the pan and set for thirty minutes in a hot oven—uncover then and cook for five minutes longer. The result is a sweet excellent for many uses—as a sauce, as a substitute for marmalade, as the foundation of pies, tarts, shortcakes, even as a filling for layer cake.

Make pies from it with two crusts, or with lattice crusts as usual. Make it into tarts, into turnovers or put between hot buttered layers for a hurry-up shortcake. But if you wish to know how excellent such rhubarb can be, make it thus into meringue pies or tarts. Bake the crusts after pricking them well, cover thinly with either good meringue or the frosting directed for cheesecakes, let it harden, then at the minute of serving cover with a thin layer of the prepared rhubarb—the meringue or frosting will stay crisp until eaten if you work quickly enough. Young unpeeled tender rhubarb gives a pink sauce—older stalks peeled furnish a translucent green. Either is sufficiently decorative. They can be made more so, if the tarts they appear on, have a cherry or preserved strawberry dropped in the middle of them.

Banana Pie: Line a deepish earthen pie dish with thin, very good crust, fill it three parts with bananas, sliced crosswise very thin. Cover them thickly with sugar, add the strained juice of a large lemon, dot with bits of butter, put on a lattice crust, and bake in a quick oven twenty-five minutes.

Banana Pudding: Slice very thin, crosswise, three medium size bananas, sprinkle thickly with sugar, then add to a batter made by beating up four egg yolks and two whites, with one cup crumbled rich stale cake, half-cup sugar, cup very rich milk, and the juice of a large lemon. Mix smooth, pour into a deep pudding dish, and bake in a quick oven, then cover with meringue made from the egg-whites left out, beaten up with a small pinch of salt, two teaspoons cold water, and six table-spoonfuls of sugar. Return to the oven and let barely color. Serve hot or cold.

Sweet Potato Pudding: Beat four eggs very light with four cups sugar and one cup creamed butter. Add a cupful of very rich milk, mix smooth, then add one pint of raw grated sweet potato. Mix well, pour into a deep earthen dish and set in hot oven. As soon as a brown crust forms on top, stir it down. Repeat this three times at least. Serve hot, with either wine sauce or a rich sugar and butter sauce, flavored with lemon. It is best not to flavor the pudding proper, so one may get

undiminished the zest of the brown crust
stirred through it.

Poor Man's Pudding: Take for each
person to be served, a fresh egg, a tablespoonful sifted flour, and half a cup very
rich milk. Add a pinch of salt for each
six eggs. Separate the eggs, beating yolks
and whites very light. Mix yolks gradually with the flour and milk, taking care
to have no lumps. Fold in the stiffly
beaten whites at the very last—if the batter is too thick add a little more milk.
Pour into a deep pan, and bake in a quick
oven. It must be taken up the moment it
is done or it will fall, and be ruined. Serve
immediately, with a sauce made by working together over hot water three cups
sugar, one cup butter, half a cup boiling
water, cup fruit juice, wine or whiskey,
with any flavoring approved. The sauce
cannot be made too rich, the pudding
should be a pale clear yellow, as light as
a puff, and cutting easily with a spoon.
It is not "true to name" in these days of
costly eggs, but deserved it in the pioneer
epoch which originated it.

Boiled Batter Pudding: Make the same batter as above, only putting in a teaspoonful baking powder. Stir well through it three cups seeded raisins, wet in whiskey and very well floured. Tie up in a newly-scalded floured pudding bag, pop in a kettle of boiling water, keep it full, with more boiling water, and cook from an hour to an hour and a half, according to size. Serve very hot with plenty of very rich sweet sauce highly flavored, and be sure to warm your knife or spoon before cutting into the pudding.

Apple Pudding: (M. W. Watkins.) Core and peel half a dozen tart apples, slice crosswise, put the slices in layers in a deep dish with plenty of sugar, butter in reason, cinnamon and a very little water. Pour over a batter made thus: one egg beaten light with half a cup sugar, butter the size of a walnut, half a cup milk, pinch of salt, flour enough to make thick enough for layer cake, with a teaspoonful baking powder sifted through. Spread batter smooth, dot with bits of butter on top, and bake in a brisk, but not scorching oven, half an hour or longer if needed—the apples must be thoroughly cooked. Serve hot or cold—preferably hot, with hard sauce or wine sauce.

Apple Dumplings: Pare and core half a dozen tart apples, stick three cloves in each, fill the core-spaces full of very sweet hard sauce, stick a sliver of mace in the sauce, then set each apple on a round of good short paste, and work the paste up over it, joining the edges neat and trig. Set close in a pan just big enough, pour around a half cup of sugar melted in a cup of water with a little butter and lemon juice. Cover the pan and cook quickly until done—then uncover, brown, take up and serve piping hot with a very rich hard sauce.

Crumb Pudding: (Anne McVay.) Soak a cup of dry grated bread crumbs in half a pint of milk until soft, add then the well-beaten yolks of two eggs, half a cup sugar, tablespoonful butter, and another half-pint milk. Flavor with lemon, vanilla or brandy, as preferred. Bake until firm in a quick, but not scorching hot oven, cover with meringue made from the egg-whites and half a cup of sugar. Barely color the meringue. Let cool, and serve with either whipped or sweetened cream, or a fruit sauce. Good without any sauce.

Blackberry Mush: (Leslie Fox.) Wash after picking a quart of fresh, very ripe blackberries, put them on with barely enough water to save from burning, bring to a good boil, and skim clean, then add gradually almost two pounds of flour, or cornstarch well wet with cold water, also sugar to taste. Cook, stirring often till the mass looks thick and glossy, pour into your pudding dish, let cool, chill thoroughly, and serve with cream either plain, or whipped, or sweetened.

Peach Pudding: Beat light one egg, with half a cup sugar, two tablespoonfuls melted butter, three-quarters cup flour, one cup sour cream, one teaspoon soda dissolved in one teaspoonful cold water, and two cups very ripe peaches, peeled and sliced thin. Bake quickly and serve when very hot with a rich hard or a wine sauce.

Ginger Pudding: Beat three eggs very

light with two cups sugar, a large cup rich
black molasses, three-quarters cup butter,
creamed, tablespoon ginger beaten fine.
Half a cup rich sour cream, half a cup
boiling water with teaspoon soda dissolved
in it, add flour enough to make a thickish
batter, pour into deep greased pan, and
bake quickly. Serve hot with rich sauce
that is flavored with some orange juice and
peel.

Nesselrode Pudding: (Mrs. H. Barker.)
Boil together three cups sugar, one cup
water until the syrup ropes. Beat it boiling hot into the yolks of six eggs previously
beaten very light. Fold in the stiffly
beaten whites, then add box Cox's gelatine
dissolved in warm water, one cup raisins,
seeded, steamed and soaked in sherry or
whiskey, one cup of nuts rolled small, else
one cup of crumbled macaroons, or a cup
of both mixed. Finish with enough thick
cream to make a full gallon, pack in salt
and ice, freeze and let stand long enough
to ripen.

Thanksgiving Pudding: (Mrs. J. O.
Cook.) Beat light the yolks of four eggs

with one cup sugar, two tablespoonfuls creamed butter, and one cup of stale cake crumbs, soaked in eight tablespoonfuls whiskey. Mix well, then add one cup raisins, seeded and floured, one cup nut meats, cut small. Beat smooth and bake until set, then cover with meringue. Serve with whipped cream or any sauce preferred. Milk can take the place of whiskey, and preserves replace raisins.

Real Christmas Pudding: Toast a pint of fine breadcrumbs to a good brown without burning, pour on them half a cup of strong, clear black coffee, and let stand till soft.

Beat six egg-yolks very light with two cups of yellow sugar and one of creamed butter, add the soaked crumbs and mix very smooth. Meantime, soak a cup of raisins, seeded and halved, a cup of clean currants, a cup of shredded citron, a cup of nut meats broken small, in a tumbler of sherry, a tumbler of rum, and wineglass of apricot brandy. Add the fruit when well soaked to the eggs and sugar, putting in any surplus liquors. Mix in gradually a teaspoonful of cinnamon, the same of cloves and allspice, half a cup of preserved ginger sliced very thin, and a very tiny dusting of black pepper and paprika. Beat smooth, then fold in the stiffly beaten egg-whites alternately with a cup of browned flour. If too thick to stir handily thin with a little milk or boiling water. Pour into a clean pudding bag, freshly scalded, leaving room for the pudding to swell, put in a deep kettle of boiling water, and boil for five hours, filling up the kettle as needed with boiling water so as not to check the cooking. Make several days beforehand, and boil an extra hour upon Christmas day. Serve in a blaze of brandy, with a very rich sauce, either fruit or wine flavored.

Pudding Sauce: (Mrs. Barbara Clayton.) Beat together until very light, one cup white sugar, one cup creamed butter, and the yolks of three eggs. Beat the egg whites very stiff with another cup of sugar, add to the yolks and butter, beat hard together, then put in double boiler and cook until thick. Put two wineglasses of good whiskey in a bowl, pour the hot sauce upon it, and whip hard until light.

Creole Cookery

Exotics rarely flower in native splendor after transplanting. Milly was the exception, proving the rule. Bred in New Orleans, steeped in its atmosphere, its traditions, a cook of degree, and daughter of a cook to whom, though past middle age, she paid the most reverent homage, she yet kept her magic touch amid the crush and hurly-burly of New York town, albeit she never grew acclimated nor even content. This in spite of a mistress she adored—in virtue of having served her ten years down in the home city. When at last Milly went back to her own, there was wailing amongst all of us, who had eaten her cook-

ing, but the mistress smiled, rather sadly,
to be sure, saying: "I could not beg her
to stay—she was so unhappy here."

Milly never had quite a free hand—New
York markets know not many things familiar to those of the Crescent City. Notwithstanding, she was a liberal education
in blended flavors, in the delights, the sur-
prises of the Creole kitchen. Tall and
slim, of a golden-brown complexion, neat
to the point of austerity, trim and self-
contained, sight of her somehow gave an
added piquancy to her dishes. She did
not make friends readily, but the comradery of cooking induced her to more than
tolerate me. "I don't say I kin cook—
but my mother can," she often told me—
smiling proudly the while, with the buzzing
praises of *gourmets* sounding in her ears.
She could never tell you how she made her
ambrosial dishes—but if you had my luck
to be *persona gratis* she could and did show
you, to the queen's taste.

I shall write only whereof I know—not
by any means a compend of Creole cookery. Indeed, a lifetime is hardly enough

to eat of all its specially excellent dishes. It seems to me from this scant experience, one general principle runs through all. It is the blending of proportioned flavors, achieved through long and gentle cooking. Milly said she let things "sob," a mistake I dare say, for the old-time "sod," past participle of "seethe." But I by no means speak with authority—my deduction is from the premise of fifty dinners, each it seemed to me uniquely excellent. After this prelude come we to specific recipes.

Court Bouillon: (Pronounced "Coubare.") Milly sighed for Redfish or Red Snapper but made shift with halibut or any other firm fine-grained fish perfectly fresh. Take three pounds of it, wash very clean, and cut in six equal slices with a very sharp knife. There must be no rags and tatters. Melt a heaping tablespoonful of lard in a deep kettle, add to it gradually two tablespoonfuls flour, stirring hard so it shall not burn. Throw into it a dozen pounded alspice, three sprigs each of thyme, parsley, bay leaf and sweet marjoram chopped fine, one small clove of garlic,

one large onion also chopped fine, and
either six large fresh tomatoes, chopped
small, or half a can—those from glass are
best. Pour in a large glass of claret, add
a quart of boiling water, and bring all to
a very brisk boil. Cook for five minutes,
then add salt and Cayenne pepper to taste.
Boil five minutes longer, then lay in the
fish slices one at a time, following them
with the strained juice of a lemon. Boil
hard twenty minutes longer. Serve hot.

To make *Court Bouillon a la Espagnole*,
stir together as above, lard and flour, taking care to have them smooth, add a large
onion, six tomatoes, clove of garlic, sprigs
of sweet basil and thyme, all chopped fine,
along with two whole bay leaves. Brown
all nicely, taking care not to burn, then add
a quart of boiling water, bring to a boil
and cook two or three minutes. Have six
thick slices of fine, firm fresh fish, rub
them well over with salt and pepper, lay
in a dish and pour over a large cup of
white wine boiling hot. Vinegar answers,
but wine is better. Lay the fish slices in
the pot, handling carefully, add the wine,

and simmer until tender—about half an hour commonly. Take up carefully so as not to break, lay in a deepish dish, remove bay leaves from the gravy and pour over the fish. Finish with a garnish of sliced lemon, and serve with either boiled rice or whole boiled potatoes.

Bouillabaisse: While time endures New Orleans will plume itself upon this dish which drew from Thackeray a world-famous tribute. "In New Orleans you can eat a Bouillabaisse, the like of which was never eaten in Marseilles or Paris." Which is much, very much, from the laureate of Bouillabaisse, as native to Marseilles. The reason of superiority is not far to seek—it lies in the excellence and flavor of the fish native to the Gulf of Mexico. Lacking Pompano, Red Snapper, and Redfish, even Milly could not quite do her knowledge justice. But she made shift with what the market offered, choosing generally halibut, with fresh cod, or bluefish, or sea trout. Two kinds of fish in equal quantity are imperative. The better, finer and firmer the fish, the better

the Bouillabaisse. Cut each sort in six
equal slices, saving trimmings, heads, etc.
Boil them in three pints of water, with a
sliced onion, and a bouquet of herbs, until
reduced to one pint. Remove fish-heads
and herbs, then strain the stock, and set
aside until needed. Meantime rub the fish
over very well with salt and pepper, then
with a mixture made by mincing very fine
three bay leaves, three sprigs each of
thyme and parsley, three cloves of garlic,
and six allspice pounded to powder. Rub
the mixture in well and thoroughly—here
is the key to success. The seasoning must
go through and through the fish. Put into
a very wide pan, two tablespoonfuls of
olive oil, heat it gently, add two mild onions, chopped and let them cook a little
without browning. Now lay in the fish,
slice by slice, so one slice does not touch
another, cover the pan, and let the slices
smother for about ten minutes, turning
them once, so as to cook each side partly.
Take up, lay separately in a large dish,
pour half a bottle of white wine into the
pan, and stir hard. Add six large, fresh

tomatoes, sliced very thin, let boil a few
minutes, then half a lemon, also in very
thin slices, and a pint of the fish stock
strained. Season well, with salt, pepper,
and Cayenne—here the palate is guide.
Boil all together until reduced almost one
half, then lay in the fish slices, taking care
they do not touch, and boil briskly for five
minutes. While the boiling goes on, chop
fine a pinch of saffron, put it in a small,
deep dish, and mix smooth with a spoonful of the boiling liquor. Dissolve the
saffron very well, and when the fish has
cooked its allotted five minutes, spread the
saffron on top of the fish. Fry in butter
as many slices of toast as you have slices
of fish—lay the fish on the toast, pour
the sauce over it, and serve immediately,
very hot.

Shrimps: The   secret   of   cooking
shrimps is to boil them properly—that is
to say in very salt water, almost brine.
They take up salt only in the boiling, and
not so much then. To five quarts of very
salt water add a large bunch of celery,
chopped, roots, leaves and all, two dozen

allspice, one dozen cloves, two blades of mace, a bouquet of herbs chopped small, a pod of red pepper, and a seasoning of Cayenne. Boil until the strength of herbs and seasoning is extracted, then throw in a hundred shrimps—river shrimps are best—let boil hard ten minutes, take from fire and allow the shrimps to cool in the brine. Serve as a relish before dinner, on a bed of cracked ice, with a garnish of parsley.

Baked Shrimp: Cut the eyes from a dozen large, meaty tomatoes, scoop out the pulp, leaving the shells whole, then mix it with one hundred shrimps boiled as directed and picked from their shells, one cup grated bread crumbs or fine cracker crumbs, and one heaping tablespoon of butter. Stew all together, seasoning with pepper and salt, fill the tomato shells with the mixture, sift fine crumbs on top, dot with butter, put in a pan, with a very little hot water in the bottom, and bake until done in a quick but not scorching oven.

Shrimp Pie: Boil and pick from shells

one hundred shrimps, mix well with two large slices stale bread free of crust, moistened with two glasses white wine, and highly seasoned with salt, pepper, Cayenne, nutmeg, mace, chopped thyme and parsley. Crisp the bread crusts, and grate over the mixture after it is packed in a deep dish. D'ot well with butter, and bake in a hot oven. Serve with a sauce made by cooking together a pint of boiled shrimps, a tablespoonful of butter, five chopped tomatoes, a little celery, thyme, parsley and bay leaf, also chopped. Cook three to four minutes, then add half a pint of oyster liquor, boil up, and serve very hot.

Shrimp Salad: Boil, and pick from shells—if large cut in half, otherwise leave whole. Season well with salt and pepper, then mix well with crisp celery, chopped fine with a very little onion. Heap in salad dish, cover with a good mayonnaise, and garnish with sliced hardboiled eggs, sliced lemon, sliced beets, and celery tips.

Fried Soft-Shell Crabs: Wash always in cold water—hot water spoils the flavor.

Remove all sand, also the sand-bag between the eyes, the apron, and the spongy growths under the side points. Rinse well again in cold water, and dry thoroughly with a clean towel. Season a pint of rich milk well with pepper and salt. Season the crabs also, lay them in the milk, rubbing them so that it may impregnate them throughout. Take out, roll in sifted flour, patting lightly as you roll, then shaking free of loose flour. Have deep fat, very hot—it must be deep enough to swim the crabs. Drop them in gently, fry to a delicate brown, skim out, drain on hot spongy paper, and serve garnished with fried parsley, and sliced lemon. Serve with Tartare sauce.

Daube: *Otherwise Beef a la Mode*: Take five pounds good lean beef, rump or top round, and lard it with a quarter pound salt pork or fat bacon, cut in thin strips and season highly with salt, pepper, onion, garlic, thyme, parsley, and bay leaves, all minced fine. Crowd in the seasoning as well as the larding strips. Make the cuts for larding three to four inches long.

Cut two large, mild onions in quarters, and put into a deep saucepan with a tablespoonful of lard, let them brown well, then lay upon them the larded beef, cover, and let simmer very slowly till well browned. When browned add five carrots and two turnips cut into inch-squares, and two more onions chopped fine. Keep covered tight, and simmer for ten minutes, then turn over the meat, and brown the other side —it will take about ten minutes more. Then cover the meat with boiling water, or weak stock, add a glass of sherry or Madeira, or even claret, season with salt, black pepper, and Cayenne to taste, then cover the pot tight, set it where it will barely simmer and let smother for three hours. The meat should be very tender. Serve hot or cold.

Cold Daube a la Creole: Lard, season, and cook, three pounds of rump or round as above directed, but keep it simmering four hours instead of three. Put into a deep dish rather large and pour over it a sauce made thus: Put a two-pound veal steak and two well-cleaned pigsfeet, in

a pot with four quarts of water, after seasoning them well with salt, pepper and
Cayenne. Add half a clove, garlic, bay
leaf, sprig thyme, one onion, all minced
fine, also two cloves pounded, and a glass
of sherry or Madeira. Keep boiling till
the meat falls from the bones—take up
then, remove bones, mince the meat fine,
season it highly and return to the liquor,
stirring it well through. Pour over the
beef, let stand uncovered in a very cool
place to harden. Serve in very thin slices
—it will be like jelly. This is a cold-
weather dish, as even an ice-box will not
harden the sauce properly in summer.

Grillades with Gravy: Flatten by beating a good round steak, and cut into
four-inch-squares. Season the squares
highly with salt, pepper, and Cayenne.
Put a heaping tablespoon of lard in a frying pan—as it melts, add a chopped onion,
a clove of garlic also chopped, and as these
brown, one tablespoonful of flour, stirring
all smooth. Next add two sliced tomatoes
with their juice—when they brown, lay the
grillades upon them. Cover close, let

them brown on one side, then turn and brown the other. Then add half a table-spoonful of vinegar, and a cup of water. Stir well, then set where it will simmer for half an hour. Fine for breakfast with hominy or rice.

Another way is to cook the grillades without garlic, and add to them along with the tomatoes half a pint of tender okra well washed and sliced. Or they can be fried brown, in clear fat, then put in a hot dish over boiling water while a gravy is made of fresh fat, heated very hot, and stirred about the pan to take up the brown meat essence, a chopped onion, two sliced tomatoes, a tablespoonful flour, as much vinegar and water. Season to taste with salt, pepper, and Cayenne, boil ten to twelve minutes and pour over the grillades.

Chicken Saute a la Creole: Clean, singe and cut in joints two spring chickens, dividing the breasts lengthwise, and cutting drumsticks from thighs. Season well with salt and pepper. Melt in a frying pan two large tablespoonfuls butter, add the chicken, and let it brown slowly for five minutes. Have three large onions sliced thin—add them and let brown but take care not to scorch in the least. Dredge in two tablespoonfuls flour, and let it brown. Then put in half a dozen large tomatoes peeled and sliced, let them brown but cook slowly, letting the pan barely simmer. Add chopped parsley, thyme and bay leaf, also two cloves of garlic finely minced, and if you have them, half a dozen sweet green peppers, freed of seed and cut in shreds. Stir well, cover and let smother for twenty minutes, stirring now and then, but keeping the pan covered. Add a cup of consommé if in hand, otherwise a cup of boiling water, cook very slowly a full half hour, seasoning to taste. After seasoning, cook ten minutes longer. Serve very hot.

Roasted Quail: Take six quail, fat, fresh and tender, pick, draw, singe, and wipe with a damp cloth inside and out. Butter inside, and sprinkle with salt and pepper lightly. Butter all over the outside, truss, and bind around with a thin slice of fat bacon. Put a tablespoonful of butter in the roasting pan, fit in the quail, and roast in a hot oven twenty to thirty minutes, according to size. Put six slices of hot buttered toast in a hot dish, and lay a quail on each. Add half a spoonful of butter, a little boiling water, and the juice of a lemon to the gravy in the pan, cook three to four minutes, stirring well, strain, set back on stove to cook two minutes longer, then pour evenly upon the breasts of the birds so it will soak in the toast. Garnish with sliced lemon and watercress, and serve with green grape jelly. If grape leaves are to be had, wrap the birds in them instead of bacon, after preparing as directed, roast, take up on toast, garnish with fresh young grape leaves, and serve with either spiced grapes or grape jelly.

Creole French Dressing: Put three tablespoonfuls of olive oil in a deep, small bowl, add to it a saltspoon salt and half one of pepper—more if taste approves. Add alternately drop by drop, a teaspoonful of made mustard, and a tablespoonful vinegar. When well mixed, add the yolk of a hard-boiled egg, mashed very smooth, and stir until blended. Serve with lettuce, celery or potato salad.

Mayonnaise Dressing: Chill a small bowl, also a fresh egg, and your salad oil. Put the yolk of the egg in the bowl—which if it is summer, should sit in cracked ice. Add drop by drop chilled oil, working it in as you drop it. When you have added a spoonful begin dropping in lemon juice, working it likewise into the yolk. It will harden the egg—stir till very hard, then add more oil, drop by drop, working it in with a fork. Repeat, until you have used the juice of half a lemon, and two gills of oil. When the egg begins to curdle add salt and pepper to taste—but do not put them in until the last. Keep and serve very cold.

Remoulade Dressing: Put three hard boiled egg-yolks into a bowl, mash smooth, add to them half a teaspoonful made mustard, one tablespoonful Tarragon vinegar, with salt and Cayenne to taste. Next add, drop by drop, three tablespoonfuls olive oil, after which put in the yolk of a raw egg, and stir until light. Finish with the juice of half a lemon, added very gradually. Much depends on the mixing—if hurried or carelessly done, the sauce will curdle. This is standard for cold meat of every sort, also heavy salads, and fish.

Drip Coffee: Two things are essential—an absolutely clean urn, and sound coffee, freshly parched, and ground neither too fine nor too coarse. The water must be freshly boiled. Put a cup of ground coffee in the strainer, pour upon it about two tablespoonfuls of boiling water, let it stand until the water drips through and there is no more bubbling, then pour on more water, but not too much, let it drip, keeping both the strainer and the spout covered to prevent the loss of aroma. Repeat until you have used almost five cups of water—this for four cups of strained coffee, as the grounds hold part of the water. Keep the pot hot while the dripping goes on, but never where the coffee will boil. If it dyes the cups it is too strong, but beware of making too weak.

Bruleau: Put into the special bruleau

bowl, which has its own brandy ladle, three ladlefuls of brandy, along with the yellow peel of half an orange, a dozen cloves, a stick of cinnamon, a few grains of alspice and six lumps of sugar. Let stand several hours to extract the essential oils. At serving time put in an extra ladleful of brandy for every person to be served, and two lumps of domino sugar. Pour alcohol in the tray underneath the bowl, light it, and stir the brandy back and forth until it also catches from the flame below. Let burn two or three minutes—if the lights have been extinguished as they should be, the effect is beautifully spectral. After the three minutes pour in strong, hot, clear, black coffee, a small cupful for each person, keep stirring until the flame dies out, then serve literally blazing hot. This "burnt water" known in more sophisticated regions as *Café Diabolique,* originated in New Orleans, and is the consummate flowering of Creole cookery.

Cakes, Great and Small

The very queen among cake makers sums her secret of success in a sentence: "The best of everything." Cake will never be better than the things whereof it is made, no matter how skilled the maker. But it can be, and too often is, dismally worse, thus involving a waste of heaven's good gifts of sugar, butter, eggs, flour and flavors. Having the best at hand, use it well. Isaac Walton's direction for the bait, "Use them as though you loved them," applies here as many otherwheres. Unless you love cake-making, not perhaps the

work, but the results, you will never excell
greatly in the fine art. Better buy your
cake, or hire the making thereof, else swap
work with some other person better gifted
in this special branch.

Here are a few cardinal helps. Have
the eggs very cold, butter soft but not oily,
flour dry and light—sun or oven-dry it in
muggy weather. Sift it three times for
ordinary cakes, twice for tea cakes, and
so on, four to five times for very light
things, sponge cake, angel's food, and
measure it before sifting, and don't forget
the needed amount—then you will be in no
danger of putting in too much or too little.
Always put a pinch of fine salt in the bottom of the mixing bowl, which ought to be
freshly scalded and wiped very dry. A
damp bowl clogs with either sugar or flour,
making the stirring much harder. Unless
specifically directed otherwise, separate
the eggs, set the whites on ice till time to
whip them, beat the yolks very, very
light—to a pale, frothy yellow, add the
sugar, free of lumps, a cupful at a time,
then the butter washed and beaten to a

creamy froth, beat hard together for five
minutes, then add alternately the flour and
the egg-whites beaten to the stiffest possible froth. Add a pinch of salt as beating begins, and if the egg supply is scant,
a teaspoonful of cold water to each white.
This will increase the quantity, and help
to make the cake lighter, as it is the air-
bubbles imprisoned in the froth which
give it its raising virtue. Add fruit and
flavoring last thing. Fruit should be well
floured but never clotted. If batter appears to be too stiff a little whiskey thins
it excellently, and helps to make it lighter.
Put in two tablespoonfuls to six eggs, using more in proportion. Rose water or
a liqueur have the same effect but give
their own flavor—which whiskey does not.

If strong butter needs must be used,
it can be mitigated to a degree, by washing
and kneading well in cold water barely
dashed with chloride of lime solution, then
rinsing well in cold water, and afterward
in sweet milk. The milk may be half
water. Rinse it out clean. Let the butter
soften well before undertaking to cream

it. A stout, blunt wooden spoon is the best for creaming, along with a deep bowl very narrow at the bottom. Grease deep cake tins plentifully, with either lard or butter—using only the best. For heavy cakes such as fruit, spice and marble cake, line them with double thicknesses of buttered paper and either set shallow pans of water in the oven while baking or stand the pans themselves in other pans with a quarter inch of water in the bottoms. If cakes brown too fast, open the oven door, a trifle, and lay over the pan a thick, well buttered paper until the oven cools. Never jar the oven while cake is baking in it—neither by banging the doors, nor dumping heavy vessels on top of it. Beware likewise slamming kitchen doors, or bumping things about in the room. Fine cake demands as many virtues of omission as of commission. Indeed the don'ts are as essential as the doings.

Layer cakes need to be mixed thinner than deep ones. The batter must run freely. Half fill the tins and set in a hot oven, taking care not to scorch before rising is finished. Butter tins very freely —it is economy in the end. Be sure the tins sit level in the oven—thus you escape an ungainly final loaf. Get filling ready as baking goes forward so as to put your layers together while still warm and pliable. Let cool before frosting, so as to trim sides smooth. Take care fillings are not too watery, also that they are mixed smooth. Spread evenly, and press down a layer firmly all over, before putting filling on top. Layers simplify greatly the problem of baking, but to my mind, no layer cake, not even the famous Lady Baltimore, is equal to a fine deep loaf, well frosted, and meltingly rich throughout.

Pound Cake: (Aunt Polly Rives) Take ten fresh eggs, their weight in fresh butter, white sugar, and thrice sifted flour. Separate the eggs, beat yolks to a creamyellow, add the sugar, cupful at a time, beat hard, then the butter creamed to a froth, then half the flour, then two wineglasses of whiskey or brandy or good sherry or rose water, beat hard five minutes, then add the rest of the flour, taking

care not to pack it in the handling. Beat
fifteen minutes longer, then fold in with
long strokes, the egg-whites beaten with
a good pinch of salt until they stick to the
dish. Barely mix them through the batter, then pour it into deep pans, or ovens,
lined with double greased papers. The
vessels also must be well buttered. Bake
with quick heat, letting the cake rise well
before browning. Slack heat when it is
a very light brown, and cook until a straw
thrust to the bottom comes out clean.
Turn out upon a thick, folded cloth, cover
with another thinner cloth, and let cool.
Frost when cool, either with the boiled
frosting directed for cheesecakes (See
Chapter on Paste, Pies and Puddings) or
with plain frosting made thus. Beat three
egg-whites well chilled to the stiffest possible froth with a pinch of salt, and a very
little cold water. Add to them gradually
when thus beaten a pound of sugar sifted
with a teaspoonful of cream of tartar. Mix
very smooth, and apply with a broad-
bladed knife, dipping it now and then in
cold water to keep the frosting smooth. It

should dry a quarter-inch thick and be delicious eating. Frosted cake keeps fresh three times as long as that left naked.

Spice Cake: Cream a coffee cup of well washed butter, with two cups yellow sugar and one cup black molasses. Add to it one after the other, seven egg yolks, beating hard between. When all are in, add one tablespoonful whiskey, or brandy, one teaspoonful grated chocolate, teaspoonful each of powdered cloves, allspice, ginger, mace, and cinnamon, a grated nutmeg, and half a saltspoonful of powdered black pepper. Add also a pinch of salt, and the barest dusting of paprika. If whiskey is for any reason disapproved, use strong, clear coffee instead, putting in two spoonfuls, and leaving out the chocolate. Beat all together hard for ten minutes, then add four scant cups flour browned in the oven but not burned. Sift after browning, adding to it two teaspoonfuls baking powder. Beat hard five minutes after the flour is all in, then pour in a deep, well greased pan, lined with buttered paper, let rise ten minutes with the oven door open, then bake in quick heat until done through.

Marble Cake: Make up egg-yolks into spice cake, beat the whites very light, and add them to three cups of sifted sugar, beaten smooth in a large cup of creamed butter. Put in a wineglass of whiskey or brandy, then add three cups and a half flour sifted three times with a heaping teaspoonful baking powder. Put the light and dark batter by alternate spoonfuls in pans well buttered and papered, let rise and bake the same as spice cake. Else bake the light and dark batter in layers, put together with any good filling, and frost with caramel frosting.

Real Gold Cake: Beat very light the yolks of sixteen eggs, with a full pound of yellow sugar, and a scant pound of creamed butter. Add a cup of rich sour cream with a teaspoonful soda dissolved in it. Or if you like better put in the cream *solus,* and add the soda dissolved in a teaspoonful of boiling water at the very last. This makes lighter cake so is

worth the extra trouble. Flavor to taste
—grated lemon rind is good. Add gradually four cups flour sifted three times at
least. Beat hard for ten minutes, then
bake in well-greased pans, lined with buttered paper, until well done, let cool partly
in the pans, then turn out, dust lightly with
flour or corn starch and frost.

Real Silver Cake: Wash and cream to
a froth a pound of fresh butter, work into
it a pound of sifted sugar, and a pound of
flour, sifted thrice with a teaspoonful of
baking powder. Add flavoring—vanilla,
lemon or rose water, following it with a
wineglass of whiskey. Then fold in the
whites of sixteen eggs beaten with a pinch
of salt to the stiffest possible froth. If the
batter looks too thick add half a cup sweet
cream—this will depend on the size of the
eggs and the dryness of the flour. Bake
in deep pans, else in layers. By baking
gold and silver batter in layers, and alternating them you can have a fine marble
cake. Or by coloring half the white batter
pink with vegetable color to be had from
any confectioner, you can have rose-mar-

ble cake. This should be iced with pink frosting else with plain white, then dotted over with pink. Very decorative for birthday parties or afternoon teas.

Christmas Cake: Prepare fruit first. Cut small half a pound of homemade citron drained from syrup, wash and seed one pound raisins, pick, wash and dry one pound currants, mince a teacup of any firm preserve—quince, peach or pear, or use a cupful of preserved cherries whole. Shred fine four ounces of homemade candied peel, also four ounces of preserved ginger, add a cupful of nutmeats—pecans or English walnuts, or even scalybarks, cutting them in bits, mix all well together, then pour upon them the strained juice of three oranges, and three lemons, also add the grated yellow peel. Next pour on half a pint of whiskey, a gill of rum, and a tumbler of cordial—peach or blackberry, and homemade if possible. Let stand overnight, in a warm place—the fruit should take up the most part of the liquor. A glass of tart jelly is held an improvement by some. I do not put it in—the preserves suit my palate better. Cream a full pound of butter with four cups sifted sugar, beat into it one at a time, ten large fresh eggs. After them put in four cups dried and sifted flour, mix smooth, then put in the fruit, drained from the liquor and lightly dredged with hot, sifted flour. Mix well, then add the liquor drained from the fruit, along with a tablespoonful of lemon essence, and as much vanilla or rose water. If the batter is too stiff to stir well, thin with either a little sweet cream or boiling water, or cordial. Pour into pans buttered and lined with five thicknesses of buttered paper, set the pans in other pans of hot water inside a warm but not brisk oven, shield the tops with double paper, and let rise half an hour. Increase heat then, but the baking must be slow. Four to five hours is required, according to the size of pans. Keep covered until the last half hour—then the heat may be sensibly increased. Test with straws—when they come out clean, take up, set pans on racks, cover with thick cloth and let cool thoroughly. Frost next day, with either plain or boiled frosting. By baking the cake in rather small square molds, set close in a larger pan, the squares can be cut without waste and frosted to make individual cakes.

White Layer Cake: (Mrs. George H. Patch.) Sift two teaspoonfuls baking powder through three and a half cups flour, measured before sifting. Cream a cup of butter with two and one half cups sugar, add a cup of rich milk, beat hard, then add gradually the flour, following it with the whites of seven eggs beaten very stiff with a small pinch of salt. Fold in lightly, and bake in three layers. Put together with orange filling, or frosting made thick with nuts and minced figs.

German Coffee Cake: (Mrs. T. G. Petre.) Beat six fresh eggs very light with one pound of sugar, and one pound flour. Add the peel of a lemon grated, and one yeast cake dissolved in a little hot milk or water. Let stand till very light, then roll into sheets one inch thick, spread them thickly with melted butter—half a pound will be required, sprinkle with two ounces bitter almonds blanched and shredded fine, mixed with four ounces sugar, and a teaspoonful powdered cinnamon. Let rise again, and bake in a moderate oven. Good hot or cold.

Cream Cake: (Betsy Vaughn.) Cream together very light two cups butter, three cups sugar, one cup sweet cream. Add gradually four cups flour sifted with one teaspoonful baking powder, then fold in the whites of fourteen eggs beaten very stiff with a pinch of salt. Flavor with bitter almonds, bake in loaves or layers, and frost with pink icing, flavored with rose water.

Sponge Cake: Beat very light the yolks of seven eggs with three cups sifted sugar, and a pinch of salt. Add to them gradually a cup of hot water, then three scant cups flour sifted thrice with two teaspoonfuls baking powder. Fold in last the stiffly beaten white of the eggs, pour into greased pans, and bake in a quick oven. The batter must not be too thin. If the eggs are large only half a cup of water may be requisite. Flavor with vanilla, putting orange or lemon in the frosting.

White Sponge Cake: Beat very stiff six egg-whites, add to them gradually a cup of sugar, and a cup of flour sifted twice with a teaspoonful of baking powder. Do not forget a tiny pinch of salt in the eggs.

Angel's Food: Beat to a stiff froth with a pinch of salt, the whites of eleven eggs. Mix in gradually a cup and a half of powdered sugar, then add a cup of flour sifted twice with a teaspoonful cream of tartar. Mix smooth, add the strained juice of half a lemon, pour into a smooth, ungreased pan, bake in a moderate oven half an hour, take up, turn pan upside down on a cloth and let stand till the cake falls out.

Chocolate Cake: Sift together two cups flour, one cup corn starch, and two teaspoonfuls baking powder, add to a cup of butter, creamed light with two cups sugar and one cup sweet cream. Add the stiffly beaten whites of seven eggs, flavor with vanilla, and bake in layers. For the filling boil together to a thick syrup, three cups sugar, one cup water, and half a cake

of grated chocolate. Pour upon three egg-
whites beaten very stiff, flavor with vanilla or bitter almond, and spread between
layers.

Orange Cake: Cream a cup of butter
with two cups sugar, beat into it a cup of
cold water, then add four cups flour thrice
sifted with two teaspoonfuls baking powder, alternate the flour with three well-
beaten eggs. Flavor to taste, bake in
layers, and put together with orange frosting made thus. Cook together till it
threads the strained juice, and grated yellow peel of a large sweet orange with one
cup sugar, then beat the hot syrup into
two egg-whites whipped as stiff as possible. Beat smooth and spread while hot.

Dream Cakes: Cream well half a cup
butter, add a cup and a half of sugar, half
a cup cold water, two cups flour sifted
twice with two teaspoonfuls baking powder, a teaspoonful lemon extract, and the
stiffly beaten whites of six eggs. Bake in
small shapes, frost, with boiled frosting,
and ornament with tiny pink candies.

Shrewsbury Cakes: This receipt with two that follow, comes down from: "The spacious days of great Elizabeth." They are given verbatim, from the original version, as it seems to me the flavor of the language must add to the flavor of the cakes. "Mix half a pound of butter, well beat like cream, with the same weight of flour, one egg, six ounces of beaten and sifted loaf sugar, and half an ounce of caraway seed. Form these into a paste, roll them thin, and lay them in sheets of tin, then bake them in a slow oven."

Queen Cakes: "Take a pound of sugar, beat and sift it, a pound of well dried flour, a pound of butter, eight eggs, and half a pound of currants, washed and picked; grate a nutmeg and an equal quantity of mace and cinnamon, work the butter to a cream, put in the sugar, beat the whites of the eggs twenty minutes and mix them with the butter and sugar. Then beat the yolks for half an hour, and put them to the butter. Beat the whole together and when it is ready for the oven, put in the flour, spices and currants, sift a little sugar over them, and bake them in tins.''

Banbury Cakes: ''Take a pound of dough, made for white bread, roll it out and put bits of butter upon the same as for puff paste, till a pound of the same has been worked in; roll it out very thin, then cut it into bits of an oval size, according as the cakes are wanted. Mix some good moist sugar with a little brandy, sufficient to wet it, then mix some clean-washed currants with the former, put a little upon each bit of paste, close them up, and put the side that is closed next the tin they are to be baked upon. Lay them separate, and bake them moderately, and afterward, when taken out, sift sugar over them. Some candied peel may be added, or a few drops essence of lemon.''

Oatmeal Cookies: (Mrs. T. G. Petre.) Beat together until creamy, one egg, half cup sugar, third cup butter, third teaspoonful soda mixed with one cup sifted pastry flour, half teaspoonful each of salt and cinnamon, then add one cup rolled oatmeal, half cup each of shredded nuts and raisins. Mix well, drop on greased tin, and bake in a slow oven. Do not let the stiffness of the dough induce you to add milk or water.

Tea Cakes: (Betsy Vaughn.) Cream together a cup and a half of butter, and two cups and a half of sugar, add to five eggs beaten very light, mix well, then add a cup and a half of buttermilk with a small teaspoonful of soda dissolved in it. Pour upon flour enough to make a soft dough, flavor with nutmeg, roll out a quarter-inch thick, cut with a small, round cutter, and bake in a quick but not scorching oven.

Tea Cakes: (M. L. Williams.) Beat five eggs very light, with five cups of sugar, a heaping cup of lard, well creamed, and two cupfuls of sour milk, with a teaspoonful of soda dissolved in it. Mix through enough flour to make a soft dough, roll half an inch thick, cut out and bake in a quick oven.

Plain Soft Gingerbread: Dissolve a desert spoonful of soda in a cup of boiling water, add to it a cup of rich molasses, along with three tablespoonfuls of melted butter. Mix well through two and and one half cups sifted flour, add ground ginger and alspice to taste, and bake in a moderate oven.

Mammy's Ginger Cakes: Beat four eggs very light with a good pinch of salt and a cup of coffee sugar. Add three cups of rich molasses, and a cup of boiling water with two teaspoonfuls soda dissolved in it. Mix well in two tablespoonfuls pounded ginger. Sift five pints of flour with a teaspoonful of salt, rub into it lightly two cups sweet lard, then add the molasses mixture and knead to a firm dough, adding more flour if needed or, if too stiff, a little sweet milk. Roll out half an inch thick, cut into big squares, bake in a quick oven, and brush over the tops while blazing hot a little butter, molasses and boiling water. Let stand in a warm place until dry. These might properly be called called First Monday Ginger Cakes, since our Mammy made them to sell upon that day to the crowds

which came to court, thereby turning many
an honest fip or picayune.

Family Gingerbread: Cup and a half
dark molasses, half cup sugar, small cup
melted lard, cup boiling water with teaspoonful soda dissolved in it, pinch of salt,
sifted flour enough to make rather stiffer
than pound cake batter. Spices to taste
—ginger, allspice, nutmeg, all in powder,
is a good mixture. Bake rather quickly.

Solid Chocolate Cake: (Mrs. R. Heim.)
Cream together one cup butter, two of
sugar, add six egg-yolks beaten light,
then add alternately one cup sour milk
with teaspoon soda dissolved in it, and
three cups sifted flour. Fold in egg-whites
stiffly beaten then add half cake Baker's
chocolate melted, and three teaspoonfuls
vanilla. Stir hard a minute, pour in deep,
well greased pan, and bake in moderate
oven.

Coffee Cake: (Mrs. R. Heim.) Beat
together until light, one egg, one cup
sugar, butter the size of a large egg. Add
alternately one cup milk, and two cups
flour with two teaspoonfuls baking powder

sifted in it. Put in pan, and sprinkle thickly all over top with sugar and powdered cinnamon. Bake rather quickly but do not scorch.

Fig Pudding: (Mrs. R. Heim.) One pound figs, half pound suet, six eggs, two cups sugar, three cups biscuit crumbs. Run figs, suet and crumbs through grinder, beat eggs very light, add other ingredients, beat again, and steam or boil in buttered mold, tied in well scalded bag, four hours. Serve hot with this sauce. Beat to a light cream, one cup butter with two cups sugar. Add two eggs very well beaten, then gradually two tablespoons vinegar and one of vanilla. Cook a long time in double boiler, stirring constantly, or it will not be smooth. Keep hot until served.

Thin Ginger Snaps: (Mrs. R. Heim.) Mix a cup of melted lard well through two of molasses, add a pinch of salt, spices to taste, and enough flour to make a soft batter. Drop by small spoonfuls on a well-greased baking sheet, and cook in quick oven.

Measure Pound Cake: (Leslie Fox.) Cream well together, one cup butter, one and three-quarter cups sugar, when very light, drop in an egg-yolk unbeaten, beat hard, put in another yolk, beat again hard, then another, and repeat the hard beating. When very light add alternately two and one-half cups flour, and one cup milk, mix well, then add half a cup flour sifted three times with three even teaspoonfuls baking powder. Follow this with the egg-whites beaten stiff. Flavor with brandy—a tablespoonful and a half. Bake in a moderate oven about an hour. Serve with any approved pudding sauce, or use as other cake. Nearly as good as the pound cake of our grandmothers.

Kisses: (Mrs. R. Heim.) Add to four fresh egg-whites unbeaten, a tiny pinch of salt, two teaspoonfuls water, and three cups fine sugar. Beat hard for at least half an hour—until the mixture is smooth and stiff. Drop from point of spoon upon buttered paper, and harden in an oven cool enough not to color.

Meat, Poultry, Game
Eggs

Barbecued Lamb: The middle piece,
known to butchers as "the bracelet," is
best for barbecuing. Have it split down
the backbone, and the rib-ends neatly
trimmed, also the ribs proper, broken
about midway, but not quite through.
Wash clean, wipe dry, rub over well with
salt, then prick in tiny gashes with a sharp-
pointed knife, and rub in well black pepper, paprika, a very little dry mustard,
then dash lightly with tabasco. Put a low
rack in the bottom of a deep narrowish
pan, set the meat upon it, letting only the

158

backbone and rib-ends touch the rack.
This puts it in a sort of Gothic arch.
Keep it so throughout the cooking. Put
a cupful of water underneath—it must not
touch the meat. Have the oven very hot,
but not scorching—should it scorch in the
least turn another pan over the meat for
the first hour of cooking. Add more water
as the first boils away, but do not baste the
meat—the water is merely to keep it from
getting too hard. Roast till the fat is
crisped and brown throughout, the lean
very tender. Take up on a broad, hot
dish, and in serving cut along the ribs,
so as to let each portion include the whole
length of them, as well as part of the
backbone. Serve with a sauce, of melted
butter, mixed with equal quantity of strong
vinegar, boiling hot, made thick with red
and black pepper, minced cucumber pickle,
and a bare dash of onion juice. This is
as near an approach to a real barbecue,
which is cooked over live coals in the bottom of a trench, as a civilized kitchen can
supply.

The middling of a pig weighing less than

a hundred pounds, well scraped, washed clean, and likewise roasted on a rack after seasoning it well, makes a fine dish. The sauce for it should include minced green peppers, instead of cucumbers. If you happen to have a pepper mango, cut it fine, and let it stand in the hot sauce ten minutes before serving.

Beefsteak with Bacon and Onions: Fry crisp a pound of streaky bacon, take up and keep warm. Make the fat bubble all over, lay in it a steak, wiped clean, seasoned with salt and pepper, and dredged lightly with flour. Sear it well on both sides—take from the fat, lay on broiler, and cook for ten minutes, turning once. Serve thus if you like it rare—if contrariwise you want it well done, set the steak on a rack or broiler in a hot oven, and let it cook there for fifteen to twenty minutes, according to thickness. Meantime dredge more flour into the fat, let it brown a minute, then lay in large, mild onions thinly sliced. Fry to a light brown, and serve around the steak. Serve the gravy separately, adding to it just before taking up, a little hot water, and shaking the pan well. This may be varied by frying with the onions or instead of them, sliced tomatoes, and green peppers finely shredded. Or cut large, very meaty tomatoes, unpeeled, into thick slices, pour off the gravy, lay them in the hot, greasy pan, season well with pepper and salt, and cook five minutes, turning them and seasoning the other side. Lay the bacon on the tomatoes— otherwise put it around the steak outside the onions.

Boned Fresh Ham: It had better not be too big—ten pounds is about the limit. Have the bone removed, but do not throw it away. Instead break it in pieces and boil them three hours in water to barely cover. Wipe the ham well inside and out, rub the inside over lightly with butter, season with salt and pepper, and pour in a little vinegar. Rub salt well over the outside and let stand on ice several hours. Make a stuffing of grated breadcrumbs, with minced pork fat, a sprig of celery chopped fine, half an apple, also chopped fine, salt, pepper, paprika, a pinch of sage in powder, and the least shred of thyme and lemon peel. A chestnut stuffing can be used, or one whose foundation is grated sweet potato. Fill the bone cavity, firmly but not too full, skewer or sew together the cut edges, and tie around twice with narrow tape. Turn over, score the skin well, rub it with soft butter or bacon fat, dredge lightly with flour, then with black and red pepper, also lightly with sugar, and lay on a low rack in a pan. Fill in sweet cider, or sound claret till it stands halfway up to the ham, cover with a close-fitting upper pan, and put into a hot oven. Cook for two hours, lifting the pan now and then, and basting the meat. Uncover, and make very, very crisp. Serve on a hot dish, with candied sweet potatoes laid around. Add boiling water to the liquor in the pan, shake it well about, and pour into a gravy boat. Or pour off the grease, add a sprinkle of flour, let it brown on top the stove, and put to it the strained liquor the bone was boiled in. Cook three minutes, and serve in the gravy boat. If the bone liquor is not used this way, make it the foundation of pea or cabbage soup. In carving cut through and through so as to serve the stuffing with each portion.

Roast Beef: Scrape and wash clean, wipe dry, sear cut sides well, either in bubbling fat, or under gas flame, set on a small rack in a deep pan, sprinkle well with salt and pepper, dredge on flour scantly, pour water underneath till it stands half an inch deep, cover close, set in a hot oven and cook until tender. Basting will not be needed until the pan is uncovered—then add a little more water, boiling hot, baste thoroughly, return to oven, and brown. If you like, add sliced tomatoes, minced onions, shredded green peppers, carrots cut small, and very tender green peas after uncovering—they will cook while the meat is browning, and can be served all together in a separate dish.

Pot Roast: Wash and dry, then brown lightly all over in hot bacon fat, and lay upon a small rack in the bottom of a deep pot, seasoning well with salt, pepper, and paprika. Pour on a little Cayenne, vinegar, add a spoonful of hot fat, then pour in enough boiling water to come half way up the meat, cover tight, and simmer until tender. An hour before serving time, put any sort of vegetables approved, or at hand, carrots, sliced, peas, string beans, lima beans, potatoes in thick slices, into the browning fat, let them cook five to ten minutes, sprinkling them well with salt and pepper, then skim out of the fat, and add to the pot, along with a cupful more boiling water. Simmer until the water is all gone, and the meat is brown. Take up, lay vegetables around the meat, or make a bed of them for it, add a little more hot water to the pot, stir well over the fire till it takes up the meat essence, then pour it over meat and vegetables, else serve in a gravy boat.

Leg of Mutton in Blanket: Make deep, narrow gashes in the thick end of a clean leg of mutton, crowd into them a mixed seasoning, salt, red and black pepper, minced onion, a little dry mustard, and powdered herbs. Brush all over with melted butter, or soft bacon fat, then sprinkle lightly with salt, set on a rack in a roasting pan, and pop into a very hot oven. Let it brown—then rub over it any tart jelly melted in a little hot water, and envelop it in a crust of flour and water, made very stiff, and rolled half an inch thick. Pinch the edges tight together, lay back in the pan, cover it, and bake in a hot oven. Take up, break the blanket carefully on top, lift out the meat, and pour the gravy from the envelop into a small sauce pan, add to it either hot claret, or a spoonful of tart jelly, along with tabasco or Worcester sauce, boil up, and serve in a boat. Tomato or walnut catsup may be used for flavoring. Indeed one sometimes finds opportunity a close second to inspiration.

The Preparation of Poultry and Game: Pick carefully, draw and singe every manner of poultry and feathered game, wash clean, quickly, in cold water, never hot, drain, then wipe as dry as possible with a soft, thick, damp cloth—it takes up moisture cleaner than a dry one. Keep very cold and away from smells until ready to cook. Tilt roasting fowls, so they may drain, if liquid gathers. Before stuffing rub over the whole inside lightly with soft butter or bacon fat, pepper it scantly, and rub on a very little salt. Grease and season the outside after stuffing is done,—never before it. If game is shot-torn, soak for ten minutes in weak salt water after plucking, rinse in cold salt water, wipe dry and drain.

Furred game, as rabbits, squirrels, possums, ought to be drawn before it is cold, if you would have the finest flavor. This is especially necessary with possums— which should be bought alive, and fattened for several weeks in a clean cage, feeding them on bread, milk, apples, potatoes, cabbage leaves, and grass. This makes them tender and much more delicate in flavor. Kill by dislocating the neck with a quick, upward jerk, then cut the throat and hang to bleed. Roll after dampening fur well in very hot embers—then scrape the same as a pig, draw, and hang to cool. Divide the skin of rabbits and squirrels around the middle, and pull off each half, the same as a kid glove. Thus no hairs stick

on the clean flesh. Draw very quickly,
wipe lightly with a damp cloth, and hang
where it is cool and airy for at least an
hour.

Roast Turkey: Make a stuffing of stale
bread. Cut the crusts from a small loaf,
grate the crumb, brown crusts crisp, crush,
sift and mix well with the gratings. Shred
finely through it four ounces fresh suet,
and a lump of butter the size of an egg.
Add a tiny heart of celery cut small, half a
tart apple also cut fine, two dozen fat
raisins, seeded, halved, and soaked for
twelve hours in whiskey to cover, salt, pepper, and paprika to taste. Mix well, stuff
the turkey but not too tight. Put a handful in the crop space, and fasten the skin
neatly over. Truss your turkey firmly,
rub all over with soft fat, then sprinkle
with salt and pepper, and set upon a rack
in a deep roasting pan, pour half an inch
of water in the bottom, cover tight, put in a
hot oven, and roast for an hour, then slack
heat and finish. The turkey will brown
thus covered, and be tenderer and sweeter
than if crisped uncovered. The pan will

hold gravy better than can be made otherwise.

Roast chickens or capons in exactly the
same way. Geese need to be roasted more
slowly and to have a seasoning of sage,
onion, and tart apple in the stuffing, instead of raisins. The dry stuffing takes
up the juices of the fowl, and is much more
flavorous, and less pasty than that which
is wet before use.

Guinea Hen in Casserole: Stick six
cloves in a cored and pared apple, thrust
a heart of celery in the core space, then
fit it inside a guinea hen, buttered, salted
and peppered inside. Pack in grated
bread crumbs—all there is space for.
Truss, grease, season, set in a hot oven,
and brown lightly all over, then lay in a
casserole on a bed of sliced carrots, young
green peas, shredded green peppers, sliced
tomatoes and tiny onions, parboiled for
five minutes. Add a large lump of butter,
rolled in flour, a cup of hot water or weak
broth, cover close, and cook an hour in a
hot oven. Serve on the vegetables, bedded

firmly, with tart jelly melted to barely run, splashed over the breast.

Chickens in Blankets: Take young fat chickens about three pounds weight, dress as for roasting, put inside each a peeled sweet potato, and a small lump of butter, after greasing and seasoning inside and out. Lay on low rack in deep pan, brown lightly in oven, then fit close over each a round of good short crust, rolled a quarter-inch thick. Return to oven—when crust is a rich brown the chickens will be done. Serve crust with each portion—thereby recalling a glorified chicken pie.

Fried Chicken: Cut into joints two tender young chickens, wipe the pieces dry, season with salt and pepper, red and black, then set on ice. Fry a pound of streaky bacon in a deep skillet, take out when crisp, roll chicken in flour, dip in beaten egg, then roll again, and lay in the fat, which must be bubbling hot, but not scorching. Cook, turning often, to a rich brown, take out, then pile in a pan, set the pan over another with boiling water in the bottom,

and put all in a very hot oven for fifteen
minutes. This cooks the chicken through
and through without making it hard. The
pieces must not touch in frying so there will
be two skilletfuls. When all the chicken
is fried, and in the oven, dredge in more
flour, stir it well through the fat, then add
a cup of cream, stirring hard all the time,
and letting it barely simmer—boiling
curdles it. Or if you want a full-cream
gravy, pour off the fat, stir the cream in
double quantity in the skillet to take up
the flavors, then pour it in a double boiler,
add pepper, salt, minced celery, a little
onion juice, and one at a time, lumps of
butter, rolled well in flour. Cook until
thick and rich, and serve in a gravy boat.

Smothered Chicken: Get two pound
broilers fat and tender, have them split
down the back, make clean, season by buttering inside and out, sprinkling with salt,
pepper and paprika, and dredging with
flour. Lay breasts down, upon a low rack
in a deep pan, cover with slices of streaky
bacon, shingling the slices well. Dredge
with pepper and flour, lay in sliced toma-

toes, shredded green peppers, and a few small parboiled onions. Add lumps of butter rolled in flour, dotting them all about the bacon. Pour in enough water to barely reach the top of the rack, cover the pan close, and cook in a hot oven, about an hour. Uncover after three-quarters of an hour, add a half-cup more water—this is for the gravy. Cover again, and finish cooking. The chickens should be brown all over but meltingly tender. Take up on a hot dish, breaking the bacon slices as little as possible. Serve the vegetables separate, also the gravy from the pan. The vegetables can be omitted, and smothered chicken still be a dish to rejoice an epicure.

Glorified Chicken Croquets: (Mrs. G. H. Patch.) Boil a large-size tender young chicken till the meat almost drops from the bones. Boil likewise tender, in salt water, one pound either sweetbreads or calf brains. Pick up the chicken and grind the meat fine, then mash it well together with the brains or sweetbreads, and season to taste. Put into a double boiler half-pint cream, tablespoonful butter, two tablespoonfuls flour, one tablespoonful parsley chopped fine, one teaspoonful onion juice, one teaspoonful salt, black and Cayenne pepper to taste. Cook smooth, stirring hard, let thicken, then add the meat, and mix thoroughly. Let cool, shape into croquets, dip in egg, roll in cracker crumbs, and fry quickly in deep hot fat.

Chicken-Turkey Hash: Cut the meat small, freeing of skin and gristle. If there is rich gravy left, put it into a skillet, and cook tender in it, half a dozen sliced tomatoes, three shredded green peppers, a small sliced onion, and a cupful of raw potato cubes. Lacking gravy, cook in butter or bacon fat, and season to taste—gravy requires less seasoning than plain fat. Add the meat, pour in a cup of boiling water, stir all well together, and cook for five minutes. Serve in a hot dish lined with thin toast. Fine for breakfast, or a very late supper.

Rabbit or Squirrel Smothered: Leave whole, rub over with fat, season highly, lay in a pan or skillet, with slices of bacon, add a cup of hot water, cover close, set over the fire, and simmer until tender. Uncover, and brown in the gravy, adding a little Cayenne vinegar at the very last.

Rabbit or Squirrel Barbecued: Leave whole, skewer flat, grease all over, lay on rack in pan, and roast in hot oven, basting every five minutes with hot salt water. When crisp, take up and serve with the sauce directed for barbecued lamb.

Quail: Smother quail the same as rabbits. I like them better halved, and fried crisp and quickly, in deep hot bacon fat. But to make the most of them, a pie's the thing. The crust must be rich and rolled a quarter-inch thick. Put in the birds whole, seasoning them well inside and out, with salt and black pepper. Put in also generous lumps of butter rolled in flour, slices of fat bacon, strips of crust an inch wide and three inches long, a little minced onion, celery or shredded green pepper if the flavors are approved, and a tiny pod of Cayenne pepper. Pour in cold water till it stands half way up the birds. Be sure the cover-crust is plenty big—pinch it down tight, prick and make a cross-cut at the center into which a tubelet of paper must be thrust to prevent the gravy's boiling over. Bake three-quarters of an hour, in a hot oven. Take up, and serve very hot. A gill of hot cream poured in through a funnel after taking up suits some palates—mine is not among them. Other folks like a wineglass of sherry made very hot.

Wild Duck: If likely to be fishy, soak an hour in vinegar and water made very salt, and roast with an onion inside stuck very full of cloves. Season inside and out, rub over with fat or butter, and roast in quick heat, to the degree required. Ducks or geese mild in flavor should be roasted with a tart apple stuck with cloves inside, also a mild onion. Rub over with fat, season with salt and pepper inside and out, and strew inside lightly a small pinch of powdered sage. A good sauce for them is made by browning half a cup of grated bread crumbs in a tablespoonful of butter, adding to it a spoonful of tart jelly, a wineglass of claret, a tablespoonful of tomato catsup, with seasoning to taste of salt and pepper.

Possum Roasted: Chill thoroughly after scraping and drawing. Save all the inside fat, let it soak in weak salt water until cooking time, then rinse it well, and partly try it out in the pan before putting in the possum. Unless he is huge, leave him whole, skewering him flat, and laying him skin side up in the pan. Set in a hot oven and cook until crisply tender, taking care there is no scorching. Roast a dozen good sized sweet potatoes—in ashes if possible, if not, bake them covered in a deep pan. Peel when done, and lay while hot around the possum, turning them over and over in the abundant gravy. He should have been lightly salted when hung up, and fully seasoned, with salt, pepper, and a trifle of mustard, when put down to cook. Dish him in a big platter, lay the potatoes, which should be partly browned, around him, add a little boiling water to the pan, shake well around, and pour the gravy over everything. Hot corn bread, strong black coffee, or else sharp cider, and very hot sharp pickles are the things to serve with him.

Eggs: Eggs demand an introductory paragraph. As everybody knows, there are eggs and eggs. An egg new-laid has a tiny air-space· at each end, betwixt the shell and the silken lining membrane. If left lying, this confined air changes its locality —leaves the ends for the upmost side of the shell. Shells are porous—through them the white evaporates—thus the air bubble on top gets bigger and bigger. By the size of it you can judge fairly the egg's age—unless it has been kept in cold storage or in water-glass. By boiling hard, throwing in cold water and peeling intact, you can see for yourself if a fresh egg so-called is truly fresh. If fresh there will be no perceptible marring of its oval—but if it shows a shrinkage, and especially if the yolk is so near the shell it shows through the cooked white, there is proof positive that the egg is not new-laid—though it may be perfectly wholesome.

Eggs kept in clean cool space do not

deteriorate under a month. Even after that, thus well kept, they answer for cake making, puddings and so on. But they have an ungodly affinity for taints of almost every kind. Hence keep them away from such things as onions, salt fish, things in brine generally, or any strong ill odors.

Duck eggs are bigger than hen eggs— eight of them being the equivalent to ten. Goose eggs run almost two for one. Turkey eggs, rarely used in cookery, are still excellent eating, much better flavored than duck eggs, which are often rather rank. Here as otherwheres, food is the determining factor. Guinea eggs, in spite of being so much smaller, are equal in raising power and in richness to hen eggs. Indeed, they are the best of all eggs for eating—rich, yet delicate. The only approach to them is the quail egg—we called it always a partridge egg—but only special favorites of the gods have any chance of ever tasting them. Quail nest frequently in wheat fields—at harvest, the uncovered nests yielded choice spoil. Daddy claimed the lion's share of it for "my white chilluns."

Often he came with his big hat-crown running over full of the delicate white ovals.
Mormonism must prevail in quail circles—
sometimes there were forty eggs in a nest.
It would have been vandalism of the worst
to eat them, only it was no use leaving
them bare to the sun, as the birds aban-
doned them unless they had begun brood-
ing. In that case the mother sat so tight,
occasionally the reaper, passing over, took
off her head. More commonly she flew
away just in time, whirring up between the
mules, with a great pretense of lameness.
If the nest by good luck was discovered in
time, grain was left standing about it.
Nobody grudged the yard or so of wheat
lost for the sake of sport.

Partridge eggs were boiled hard, and
eaten out of hand—they were much too
thin-shelled for roasting, in spite of having a very tough lining membrane. With
guinea eggs there was quite another story.
They have shells extra thick and hard—
hence were laid plentifully in hot ashes,
heaped over with live coals and left as long
as our patience held out. When Mammy

pulled them out, it was maddening to see her test them. She laid a short broom straw delicately on each egg. If it whirled round, the egg was done—if contrariwise it fell off, it had to go back in the embers. She had no thought of letting us eat eggs not cooked till the yolk was mealy. To this day I am firmly of opinion she was wise—and right. Eggs roasted as she roasted them have a flavor wholly beyond and apart from those cooked in any other way.

Baked Eggs: These most nearly approximate the flavor of roasted ones. Break fresh eggs at the small ends, drain away the whites, break down the shells to deepish cups, each with a yolk at bottom, sprinkle yolks lightly with salt and pepper, add a bit of butter to each, then set shells upright, close over the bottom of a pan, pop the pan into a hot oven, bake twenty minutes, and serve piping hot. This Mammy gave us to keep from wasting yolks when wedding or Christmas cake demanded many whites for frosting.

Potato Egg Puffs: Into a quart of rich

and highly seasoned mashed potatoes, beat two eggs, then divide into equal portions— six or eight. With lightly floured hands make each portion into a ball, set the balls in a baking dish, then press into each a hard-boiled egg. Lay a bit of butter on each egg, and dredge lightly with salt and pepper. Bake in a quick oven until the potato is brown and light—it ought to rise up like a fat apple.

Egg Dumplings: Cousins-germane to the puffs but richer—will serve indeed for the meat course of a plain dinner. Mix the potato well with half its bulk of finely chopped cold meat, the leaner the better, bind with beaten eggs, then divide and roll each portion around a hard-boiled egg, lay the dumplings in a greased and floured pan, giving them plenty of room, pour around them a good gravy, or else a rich tomato sauce, then bake ten to twenty minutes in a hot oven.

Egg Spread: Spread a flat pan an inch deep with rich mashed potato, sprinkle with pepper and salt, then cover the top with eggs hard boiled, and cut in half.

Set them yolk up. Put salt, pepper and butter on each yolk, and bake ten minutes in a warm oven. Or if soft eggs are preferred, make depressions in the potato with the back of a spoon, break an egg in each, dust with pepper and salt, add a dot of butter and bake five minutes. If the potatoes are wanted brown, bake them ten minutes after making the depressions, then put in the eggs and bake soft or hard at will.

Poached Eggs: These require a deep skillet, three parts full of water on the bubbling boil, which is slightly salted and well dashed with vinegar. Break all the eggs separately before putting one in. Slip them in, one after the other, quickly, taking care not to break yolks, keep the boiling hard, and use a knife or spoon to prevent the whites from cooking together. Take out in six to seven minutes, using a skimmer and draining well, trim rags off white, lay in a deep hot dish, and pour over real melted butter, made with butter, hot water, salt, pepper, lemon juice or vinegar, and a dash of tabasco. Send to table covered—a poached egg chilled has lost its charm. Or you may serve the eggs on squares of hot, well-buttered toast, which have been sprinkled thickly with grated cheese, then set for a minute inside a hot oven. Served thus, pass the melted butter with them, as if poured over, they might be too rich for some palates.

Egg Fours: Cut hard-boiled eggs in four lengthwise, mix yolks with an equal bulk of sardines, drained, freed of skin and bone, and minced fine. Season with salt, pepper, lemon juice, or vinegar, and olive oil. Add minced olives if you like. The mixture must be soft, but not too soft to shape well. Shape it into small ovals, using two spoons, and lay an oval in each quarter of the whites. Put very narrow strips of pimento on the ovals, then sprinkle them thickly with grated cheese—Edam is good for such use. Set in a baking dish and cook two to four minutes in a hot oven. If wanted extra tasty, as for a relish before dinner, set the fours on narrow strips of toast, spread with made mustard, well-mixed with finely minced very sour cucumber pickle.

Bacon sliced thin, fried crisp without scorching, and finely minced can take the place of sardines. Indeed, in making fours the widest latitude prevails—you can vary flavors and proportions almost infinitely. Onion, even a suspicion of garlic, tabasco, Cayenne vinegar, walnut catsup, or Worcester can be added. Capers mixed through the mass make it wonderfully piquant. But things which need to be crisply fresh, such as celery and lettuce, must be let severely alone.

Stuffed Eggs: Staple for picnics, and barbecues. Boil twenty minutes, throw instantly in cold water, and shell immediately. Halve, mash yolks while hot with a plentiful seasoning of butter, pepper, salt, a little onion juice, capers or bigger pickle finely minced, and pimentos cut small. Work the seasoning well through, then shape into balls yolk-size, put each between two half-whites, and fasten together with a couple of tooth picks. Wrap each as finished in wax paper, and keep cool until needed. Here may be a good place to say that the quicker a hard-boiled egg is got out of its shell after chilling, the better and more delicate will be its flavor.

Fried Eggs: Anybody, almost, can fry an egg wrong. It takes some skill to fry one exactly right. Have the frying pan covered with grease, hot, but not scorching, slip in the eggs, previously broken separately, taking pains not to break yolks, sprinkle lightly with salt and pepper, keep edges from running together, then when they have hardened underneath, dip hot grease over the tops, keeping on till the white sets. If the heat is right the eggs will not stick to the pan. Cook as hard as is desirable, take up with a cake-turner, and lay in a shallow pan, lined with soft clean paper. Keep hot while they drain— it takes a minute or so—then remove to a blazing hot dish, and serve. If ham goes with them lay it in the middle, with eggs all around it. Triangles of fried toast in between look and taste well at breakfast.

Soups, Salads, Relishes

Vegetable Soup: Cut into joints two fat chickens three parts grown, salt and pepper, and lay aside while you fry in a deep pot half a pound streaky bacon. Take out when crisp, put in the chicken, turning it so as to brown it all over. Put in a thick slice of ham, let it also brown a bit, do the same with four sliced onions— mild ones—then add two gallons cold water, half a teaspoonful salt, two pods red pepper, a dozen whole pepper corns, and two sprigs of parsley. Keep at a gentle boil for an hour, then put in two small heads of tender cabbage finely shredded, and six white potatoes, peeled and sliced a quarter-inch thick. Fifteen minutes later put in a quart of string beans, broken short, a pint of shelled lima beans, a stalk of celery cut fine lengthwise, and a dozen tomatoes, peeled and sliced. Follow them in ten minutes with a pint of tender okra sliced—next add a little later the pulp from a dozen ears of green corn, slit lengthwise and scraped. Stir almost constantly with a long-handled skimmer, after the corn pulp is in. If the skimmer brings up chicken bones, throw them aside. Just before serving put in a large spoonful of butter, rolled in flour. Taste, add salt if required. Serve very hot with corn hoe cake and cider just beginning to sparkle. If there is soup enough for everybody, nothing else will be wanted.

Black Turtle Bean Soup: Pick and wash clean, one quart black turtle beans, soak overnight in three quarts cold water, and put on to boil next morning in the soaking water. When it boils add three onions sliced, one carrot scraped and cut up, a stalk or so of celery, three sprigs of parsley, and one tomato, fresh or canned. Boil slowly four to five hours, until the beans are tender, filling up with cold water as that in the kettle wastes. When the beans are very soft, strain all through a fine collander, mashing through beans and vegetables, add a quart of very good soup stock, also a bay leaf, and boil up hard half a minute before serving. Put into each soup plate a slice of lemon, a slice of hard-boiled egg, and a tablespoonful of sherry wine before adding the soup.

Gumbo: Cut a tender, fat chicken, nearly grown, into joints, season well with salt and pepper, and fry for ten minutes in the fat from half a pound of bacon, with two thick slices of ham. Then add two onions chopped fine, six large ripe tomatoes, peeled and chopped, adding with them their juice, half a large pod of mild red pepper, cut small, a teaspoonful of minced thyme and parsley mixed, a pint of tender sliced okra, stemmed and cut lengthwise. Cook altogether, watching all the time, and stirring constantly to prevent scorching until everything is well-browned. Then add three quarts fresh-boiled water, on the full boil, set the pot where it will barely

simmer, and cook an hour longer, taking
the same pains against scorching. Rice to
eat with the gumbo—it must never be
cooked in the pot—needs to be washed until
the water runs clear from it, drained, then
tossed into a wide kettle of water on the
bubbling boil, and cooked for twenty minutes. The water must be salted to taste.
Drain the rice in a collander, set it after
draining in the oven for a minute. The
grains should stand out separate, but be
very tender. Rice thus cooked, and served
with plenty of butter, is excellent as a
vegetable.

Wedding Salad: Roast unstuffed, three
young tender turkeys, or six full grown
chickens. Take the white meat only, cut
it fine with shears, cutting across the grain,
while hot. Let cool, then mix it with ten
hearts of crisp celery cut in bits, two heads
of tender white cabbage, finely chopped,
rejecting hard stalks—use three heads if
very small—and set in a cool place. For
the dressing boil thirty fresh eggs twenty
minutes, throw in cold water, shell, take
out the yolks, saving the white for garnish-

ing, mash the yolks while hot very smooth
with a pound and a half of best butter,
season them well with salt, pepper, a little
dry mustard, celery seed, and, if at hand,
a dash of walnut catsup, but not enough
to discolor. Add also a teaspoonful of
sugar—this to blend flavors only. Add a
little at a time enough warm vinegar to
make as thick as cream. Chill, and pour
over the salad, mix well through, then heap
it in a big glass bowl, lined with partly
white lettuce leaves, make a wreath of
leaves around the top, and in serving, lay
a larger lettuce leaf on each plate, filling
it with the yellow-white salad.

Fruit Salad: Wash well a very ripe
juicy pineapple, let dry, then shred with a
fork, holding the crown in the left hand
firmly, while you pull away sections with
the fork in the right. Thus you avoid taking any of the hard center. Peel the sections delicately after they are separated,
and cut them in long thin slivers, with the
grain. Arrange these slivers star-shape
upon lettuce leaves in the plates, lay a very
narrow slip of pimento—sweet red pepper,

—between each two of them, then fill in the points of the stars with grape-fruit pulp, freed of skin and seed, and broken into convenient sized bits. Lay more pimento strips upon it. Set on ice till ready to serve, then drench with sweet French dressing.

Sweet French Dressing: Mix well a scant teaspoonful of granulated sugar, the same of dry mustard, half a teaspoonful salt, as much black pepper and paprika mixed, put in the bottom of a deep small bowl, and stir for two minutes. Wet with claret vinegar, adding it gradually, and stirring smooth. Make as thick as cream. Add twenty drops tabasco, twenty drops onion juice, the strained juice of half a lemon, and half a teaspoonful of brandy, rum or whiskey. Mix well, then add, tablespoonful at a time, a gill of salad oil, stirring hard between spoonfuls. Put in more vinegar, more oil—the seasoning suffices for half a pint of dressing. Stir till it thickens—it should be like an emulsion when poured upon the salad. Keep on ice. The oil and vinegar will separate, but the dressing can be brought back by stirring hard.

Banana and Celery Salad: Chill heart celery and very ripe bananas, slice thin crosswise, mingling the rounds well. Pile on lettuce leaves, and cover with French dressing, into which finely grated cheese has been scantly stirred. This dressing with cheese is fine for tender Romaine, also for almost any sort of cooked vegetable used as salad.

Red and White Salad: Make cups from lettuce hearts, fasten them to the plate, with a drop of melted butter, fill lightly with grape-fruit pulp, and set a tiny red beet, boiled tender, in the middle. Have a very sharp French dressing made with oil lemon juice and Tarragon vinegar. Pass with this cheese straws, or toasted cracker sprinkled lightly with Parmesan cheese.

Pineapple Salad: Pare and core a very ripe, sweet pineapple, cut in slices crosswise, lay the slices in a bowl, with a sprinkle of sugar, half a cup rum or sherry, all the juice shed in cutting up, and a grate of nutmeg. Let stand till morning, cool, but not on ice. Make rosettes of small lettuce leaves in the plates, lay a slice of pineapple on each, fill the hole in the center with pink pimento cheese. Make the cheese into a ball the size of a marble, and stick in it a tiny sprig of celery top. Put a little of the syrup from the bowl in each plate, then finish with very sharp French dressing. Make the pimento cheese by grinding fine half a can of pimento, and mixing it through two cakes of cream cheese, softening the cheese with French dressing, and seasoning it to taste.

Cold Slaw: (V. Moroso.) Shave very fine half a medium sized head of tender cabbage, put in a bowl, and cover with this dressing. Melt over hot water a heaping tablespoonful of butter, with two tablespoonfuls sugar, a saltspoon of pepper, a teaspoonful of salt, dash of red pepper, and scant teaspoonful dry mustard. Mix smooth, then add gradually four tablespoonfuls vinegar, mix well, then put in the yolk of a raw egg, beating it in hard. Cook till creamy, but not too thick. Take

from fire, and add if you like, two tablespoonfuls cream, but it is not essential—
the dressing is good without it.

Tomato Soy: Take one gallon solid,
ripe tomatoes, peeled and sliced, or four
canfuls put up in glass, put in a preserving kettle with a quart of sliced onions,
two tablespoonfuls salt, as much moist
sugar, teaspoonful black pepper, saltspoon
paprika, four hearts of celery cut fine, a
tablespoonful of pounded cloves, alspice,
mace, grated nutmeg, and cinnamon mixed.
Stir well together and cook slowly, taking
care not to burn, until reduced one-half.
Dry mustard or mustard seed can be
added, but many palates do not relish
them. After boiling down add a quart of
very sharp vinegar, stir well through,
skim if froth rises, bottle hot, and seal.
This keeps a long time in a dark cool place.

Table Mustard: Mix well together two
tablespoonfuls dry mustard, scant teaspoon sugar, half a teaspoon salt. Wet
smooth, to a very stiff paste with boiling
water, then add either a teaspoon of onion
juice, or a clove of garlic mashed, stir well

through, add little by little, a tablespoonful olive oil, then thin, with very sharp
vinegar, added gradually so as not to lump
nor curdle, to the consistency of thin
cream. Put in a glass jar, seal tight and
let stand a week. A month is better—indeed, the mustard improves with age if not
permitted to dry up.

Cabbage Pickle: Shred enough tender
cabbage to make four quarts, put with it
four large green tomatoes, sliced thin, six
large onions, chopped fine, three green
peppers also chopped, rejecting the seed,
two ounces white mustard seed, half-ounce
celery seed, quarter-ounce turmeric, three
tablespoonfuls salt, two pounds white
sugar, two quarts vinegar. Put all in a
preserving kettle, set it upon an asbestos
mat over a slow fire, and cook gently for
several hours, stirring so it shall not
scorch. It must be tender throughout but
not mushy-soft.

Cauliflower Pickle: Drop two heads
cauliflower in salted boiling water, cook
fifteen minutes, take up, drop in cold water,
separate into neat florets, and pack down

in a clean crock. Pour upon the florets, hot, a quart of vinegar, seasoned with a mixture of two tablespoonfuls salad oil, teaspoonful dry mustard, tablespoonful sugar, teaspoonful salt, half-teaspoonful onion juice, half-teaspoonful black pepper, dash of paprika, ten drops tabasco. Bring all to a boil, and pour over the pickle, first strewing well through it blade mace, whole cloves, alspice and cinnamon, broken small but not powdered.

Pear Relish: Wash and stem a gallon of sound ripe, but not mellow Seckel pears, remove the blossoms with a very sharp narrow pen-knife, and stick a clove in each cut. Drain, and drop into a syrup, made of three pounds of sugar and a quart of vinegar. Bring to a quick boil, skim, and set back to simmer. Add after skimming, cloves, alspice, mace, ginger, cinnamon, and black pepper, pounded small but not powdered. Cut up a large sweet red pepper, and drop in the shreds. Let cook till the pears are tender. If the syrup is thin, add more sugar—some pears yield more juice than others. Sliced lemon gives a piquant tang, but is optional. Put in glass or stone jars, and cover tight, laying a brandy paper on top.

Cherries Piquant: Wash well, and stem but do not pit, half a gallon ripe Morello cherries. Drain well, strew spices well through them, lay thin sliced lemon on top, add a dozen whole pepper corns, and a tiny pod of Cayenne pepper, then pour over a pint of sharp vinegar, boiled with four pounds of sugar, and skimmed clean. Let stand all night, drain off syrup in the morning, boil up, skim, and pour again over the fruit. Next day, put all in a kettle, and cook for fifteen minutes, then put in glass jars, seal and keep dark. Especially good with game or any meat highly seasoned.

Gooseberry Jam Spiced: Wash, and nub half a gallon of green gooseberries, picked just before they ripen. Put them in a kettle with six large cups of sugar, a cup of water, half a teaspoonful each of cloves, alspice, mace, grated nutmeg, and cinnamon, the grated yellow peel of an orange and the strained juice. Cook slowly until thick—it should jelly when dropped on a plate. Pack in small jars. One of the very finest accompaniments to any sort of fowl. By leaving out the spices, and merely cooking the berries thick enough to cut like cheese, it is as fine as *bar le duc* for serving with salad.

Frozen Cranberry Sauce: (Mrs. R. Heim.) Gives a new tang to game, roast turkey, capon or duck. Cook a quart of cranberries until very soft in one pint water, strain through coarse seive, getting all the pulp, add to it one and a half pints sugar, the juice—strained—of four lemons, one quart boiling water, bring to a boil, skim clean, let cool, and freeze rather soft.

"Apple Sauce Gone To Heaven": Thus a poet names it, though I, the architect thereof, insist that it is wholly and beautifully mundane. To make it, pare eight firm apples, the higher-flavored the better, core, drop into cold water, as pared, let stand till you make the syrup. Take a cup of sugar to each two apples and a cup of water to each two cups of sugar. Bring to a boil, skim, clean twice, then throw in

half a dozen blades of mace, bits of thin yellow peel from two lemons, a few bits of stick cinnamon, and one pepper corn—no more. Stick four cloves in each apple, drop them in the syrup, which must be on the bubbling boil. After the apples are in —they should just cover the pan, add the strained juice of two lemons. Boil hard for five minutes, turn over the apples, simmer till done—they will look clear all through. Skim out with a perforated ladle, letting all syrup drain away from them, arrange in a deepish glass dish, or pile on a glass platter. Boil the syrup until it jellies when dropped on a plate, then dip it by spoonfuls over the apples, letting it harden as it is dipped.

Another way, and easier, is to wash and core the apples, without peeling, stick in the cloves, put in an earthen or agate baking dish, add the sugar, water, spices, cover close, and set in a hot oven. Cook until the apples are soft through, then uncover, and crisp a little on top. The peel will be edible, and the flavor richer than when boiled, but the dish is not so decorative.

Spiced Grapes: Wash and drain sound full-ripe grapes, pick from the stems, then pop out the grapes singly from the hulls. Save the hulls and juice. Put the pulp and seeds over the fire, cook until soft, strain through a colander to remove the seed, then add the pulp to the hulls and juice, put all over the fire, with equal weight of sugar, and spices to taste. I like cloves, alspice, mace and cinnamon, all pounded small, but not powdered. Cook until thick, take care not to burn, put into glasses like jelly, and serve with any sort of meat, or as a sweet.

Wild grapes washed, picked from stems, stewed and passed through a colander, furnish a pulp that is worth sugar, spices and so on. Cook as directed for vineyard grapes. By leaving out the most part of spices, and putting in vinegar, a cupful to the quart of syrup, the result is a very piquant jelly, or more properly, fruit cheese.

Sweet-Sour Pears: The pears must be ripe, but very firm. If large, pare and quarter, cutting out the core, stick a clove in each quarter, and drop as pared in cold ginger tea. If small or medium, wash instead of paring, take out cores, stick two cloves in each cavity, pack close in the kettle and cover when all are in with strained ginger tea. Boil in the tea fifteen minutes, until a fork will pierce without too much exertion. Skim out then, pack in jars, strewing spices liberally through, then cover with vinegar boiling hot, to which you had added a cupful of sugar for each quart. Let stand twenty-four hours, drain off, boil, and pour over again. Do this three times, then put all in the kettle, bring to a boil, cook five minutes, and put while hot in clean stone jars.

Spiced Plums: All manner of plums, even the red wild fruit, make the finest sort of relishes when cooked properly. Wash, pick, and weigh, take four pounds of sugar to five of fruit, with what spices you choose, never forgetting a tiny pod of Cayenne pepper, put all over the fire, let boil slowly, skimming off froth. Stir with a perforated skimmer—it will take out the most part of stones. A few stones left in give a fine bitter almond flavor after the plums have stood a while. Take care not to scorch, cook until very thick, then add strong vinegar, a cupful to the half-gallon of fruit. Boil three minutes longer, put hot into well-scalded jars, lay brandy paper over, or seal with paraffin.

Baked Peaches: Especially fine with barbecued lamb or roast duck or smothered chicken. Peel one dozen large, ripe, juicy peaches, stick two cloves in each, set in an agate or earthen pan they will just fill, add two cups sugar, a tablespoonful butter, a very little water, and a good strewing of mace and lemon peel. Cover close, and bake until done. Serve hot. Instead of butter, a gill of whiskey may be used, putting it in just before the peaches are taken up, and letting them stand covered until the spirit goes through them. So prepared, they are better cold than warm. The pits flavor the fruit so delicately they should never be removed.

Vegetables, Fruit Desserts, Sandwiches

Tomato Layer: Peel and slice a dozen
meaty tomatoes, slice thin six mild onions,
cut the corn from half a dozen large ears,
saving the milk. Cover an earthen baking
dish with a layer of tomatoes, season well
with salt and pepper, also the least suspicion of sugar. Lay onion slices over,
sprinkle lightly with salt, then add a layer
of corn, seasoning it with salt and a little
sugar. Repeat till the dish is full. Pour
over the corn milk, the tomato juice, and
a heaping tablespoonful of melted butter.
Bake in a hot oven half an hour, covering

it for twenty minutes, then browning uncovered. When corn is not in season, very crisp brown bread crumbs may take its place. But it should be against the law to put soft crumbs or any sort of bread uncrisped, into cooked tomatoes. A green pepper shredded and mixed through the layers adds to the flavor—for the devotees of green peppers.

Corn Pudding: Slit lengthwise the grains in eight large ears of corn, scrape out the pulp carefully, saving all milk that runs. The corn should be full, but not the least hard—if it has reached the dough state, the grains will keep shape. Beat three eggs very light, with half a teaspoonful salt, a tablespoonful sugar, plenty of black pepper, and paprika, half a cup of very soft butter, and half a cup sweet cream. Add the corn pulp and milk, stir well together—if too thick, thin with a little milk. Pour into a pudding dish, cover and bake ten minutes, then uncover, and bake until done.

Fried Corn: Fry crisp, half-pound streaky bacon, take up, and put into the fat, bubbling hot, eight large ears of corn cut from the cob, and seasoned with salt and black pepper. Add also the corn-milk, stir well together for five minutes, then put an asbestos mat under the skillet and let stand till the corn forms a thick brown crust over the bottom. Pour out, loosen this crust with a knife, lay on top the corn, lay on also the crisp bacon, and serve very hot. A famous breakfast dish down south all through ''Roas'in' ear time.'' That is to say, from July to October.

Hulled Corn: Known otherwise as lye hominy, and samp. Put a pint of clean strong wood ashes into half a gallon of water, boil twenty minutes—or until the water feels slippery. Let settle, drain off the clear lye, and pour it upon as much white flint corn, shelled and picked, as it will cover. Let stand until the hulls on the grains slip under pressure—commonly twelve to twenty-four hours. Drain off lye, cover with cold water, rubbing and scrubbing the grains between the hands, till all are free of husks. Soak them in clear water, changing it every few hours till no taste of lye remains. Then boil slowly in three times its bulk of water, adding a little salt, but not much, until very tender. A grain should mash between finger and thumb. Fill up as the water boils away, and take care not to scorch. Cool uncovered, and keep cool. To cook, dip out a dishful, fry it in bubbling bacon fat as directed for corn. Or warm in a double boiler, and serve with butter and sugar or cream and sugar, as a cereal. Use also as a vegetable the same as rice or green corn. Hominy pudding, baked brown, and highly seasoned, helps out a scant dinner wonderfully, as corn is the most heating of grains, as well as one of the most nutritious.

Steamed Potatoes: Wash clean a dozen well-grown new potatoes, steam until a fork will pierce, dry in heat five minutes, then peel, and throw into a skillet, with a heaping tablespoonful of butter, well-rolled in flour, half a pint of rich milk, ten drops onion juice, salt and pepper to taste, and a teaspoonful of chopped parsley.

The sauce must be bubbling when the potatoes are put in. Toss them in it for five minutes, put in deep dish and pour the gravy over. Serve very hot.

Candied Sweet Potatoes: Boil medium potatoes of even size, till a fork will pierce —steaming is better though a bit more trouble—throw in cold water for a minute, peel, and brush over with soft butter, then lay separately in a wide skillet, with an inch of very rich syrup over the bottom and set over slow fire. Turn the potatoes often in the syrup, letting it coat all sides. Keep turning them until candied and a little brown. If wanted very rich put butter and lemon juice in the syrup when making it. Blade mace also flavors it very well.

Tipsy Potatoes: Choose rather large potatoes, peel, and cut across into round slices about half an inch thick. Pack these in a baking dish with plenty of sugar, and butter, mace, yellow lemon peel, pounded cloves, and a single pepper corn. Add half a cup boiling water, cover and bake till a fork pierces, then uncover, add a

glass of rum, and keep hot, but not too
hot, until serving time. Or you can use
half a pint of claret, instead of the boiling
water. Still another way, is to mix a glass
of sherry with a spoonful of cream, and
add it to the dish five minutes before it
goes to table. Sweet cider can take the
place of wine. So can lemon or orange
juice. But to my thinking, the Demon
Rum, or his elder brother whiskey, is best
of all.

Left-over Sweet Potatoes: Peel, slice
thick, dip in melted butter, roll in sugar
well seasoned with grated lemon peel,
and nutmeg, lay in a pan so as not to
touch and make very hot in the oven.
This last estate is always better than the
first.

Potato Balls: Mash boiled or baked
sweet potatoes smooth, seasoning them
well with salt, pepper, cinnamon, a little
nutmeg, and melted butter. Bind with a
well-beaten egg, flour the hands, and roll
the mashed potato into balls the size of
large walnuts. Roll the balls in fine
crumbs or sifted cornmeal, drop in deep

hot fat, fry crisp, drain, and use as a garnish to roast pork, roast fowl, or broiled ham.

Bananas: Bananas are far too unfamiliar in the kitchen. They can be cooked fifty ways—and in each be found excellent. The very best way I have yet found, is to peel, slice in half, lengthwise, lay in a dish with a cover, shake sugar over, add a little mace, lemon juice, lemon peel, and melted butter, then bake until soft—seven to fifteen minutes in a hot oven, according to the quantity in the dish. Or peel and slice, leave unseasoned, and lay in the pan bacon has been cooked in, first pouring away most of the fat. Cook five minutes in a hot oven, and send to table with hot bread, crisp bacon and coffee for breakfast. A thick slice of banana, along with a thick slice of tart apple, both very lightly seasoned, makes a fine stuffing for squabs. Half a banana delicately baked, and laid on a well-browned chop adds to looks and flavor.

Baking Vegetables: Paper bags taught me the ease and value of cooking vegetables in the oven rather than on top the stove. Less care is required, less water, rather less heat. Peas and lima beans, for example, after shelling, should be well washed, put in a pan with salt, seasoning and a little water, covered close, and baked in a hot oven half an hour to an hour. Green corn is never so well cooked, outside a paper bag, as by laying it on a rack in a covered pan, putting a little water underneath, covering close and setting the pan for nine minutes in a hot oven. It is sweeter and richer than even when put in cold unsalted water, brought to a boil, cooked one minute, then taken up. But however heat is applied, long cooking ruins it. Cook till the milk is set—not a second longer. Green peas should have several tender mint leaves put in with them, also sugar in proportion of a teaspoonful to half a pint of shelled peas. Lima beans are better flavored if the butter is put with them along with the water. Use only enough to make steam—say two table-spoonfuls to a fair-sized pan. Spinach and beet greens also bake well, but require

more water. Leave out salt, adding it
after draining and chopping them. They
take twenty to thirty minutes, according
to age.

All manner of fruits, berries in especial,
cook finely in the oven. Put in earthen
or agate ware, with sugar, spices and a
little water, cover close and cook half to
three quarters of an hour, according to
bulk. Uncover then—if done take up, if
not let cook uncovered as long as needed.
Set the baking dishes always on rack or
a grid-shelf, never on the oven bottom nor
solid metal. Thus the danger of burning
is minimized, also the need of stirring.

For *cauliflower au gratin,* cut the head
into florets, lay them compactly in the
baking dish, add a little water, with salt,
pepper and butter. Bake covered until
tender, then shake over the grated cheese,
and set back in the oven three to five minutes. Tomatoes, peeled and whole except
for cutting out the eyes, baked in a dish
with a liberal seasoning of salt, pepper,
and butter, a strewing of sugar and a little
onion juice, look and taste wholly un-

like stewed tomatoes, common or garden variety.

Boiling with Bacon: Get a pound of streaky bacon, cut square if possible, scrape and wash clean, put on in plenty of water, with a young onion, a little thyme and parsley, bring to a quick boil, throw in cold water, skim the pot clean, then let stand simmering for two to three hours. Add to it either greens—mustard, turnip, or dandelion or field salad, well washed and picked, let cook till very tender, then skim out, drain in a colander, lay in a hot dish with the square of bacon on top. Here is the foundation of a hearty and wholesome meal. The bacon by long boiling is in a measure emulsified, and calculated to nourish the most delicate stomach rather than to upset it. Serve two thin slices of it with each helping of greens. You should have plenty of Cayenne vinegar, very hot and sharp, hot corn bread, and cider or beer, to go along with it.

String beans, known to the south country as snaps, never come fully to their own, unless thus cooked with bacon. Even pork does not answer, though that is far and away better than boiling and buttering or flooding with milk sauces. It is the same with cabbage. Wash well, halve or quarter, boil until very tender, drain and serve. Better cook as many as the pot will hold and the bacon season, since fried cabbage, which is chopped fine, and tossed in bacon fat with a seasoning of pepper, salt and vinegar, helps out wonderfully for either breakfast, luncheon or supper. Never throw away proper pot-liquor—it is a good and cheap substitute for soup on cold days. Heat, and drop into it crisp bread-crusts—if they are corn bread crusts made very brown, all the better. Pioneer folk throve on pot-liquor to such an extent they had a saying that it was sinful to have too much—pot-liquor and buttermilk at the same meal.

Fruit Desserts: Fruits have affinities the same as human beings. Witness the excellent agreement of grape fruit and rum. Nothing else, not the finest liqueur, so brings out the flavor. But there are other fruits which, conjoined to the grape fruit, make it more than ever delicious. Strawberries for example. They must be fine and ripe. Wash well, pick, wash again, halve if very large, and mix well in a bowl with grape fruit pulp, freed of skin and seed, and broken to berry size. Add sugar in layers, then pour over a tumbler of rum, let stand six hours on ice, and serve with or without cream.

Strawberries mixed with ripe fresh pineapple, cut to berry size, and well sweetened, are worthy of sherry, the best in the cellar, and rather dry than sweet. Mixed with thin sliced oranges and bananas, use sound claret—but do not put it on until just before serving—let the mixed fruits stand only in sugar. Strawberries alone, go very well with claret and sugar—adding cream if you like. Cream, lightly sweetened, flavored with sherry or rum, or a liqueur, and whipped, gives the last touch of perfection to a dessert of mixed fruit, or to wine jelly, or a cup of after-dinner coffee, or afternoon chocolate.

A peach's first choice is brandy—it must be real, therefore costly. Good whiskey answers, so does rum fairly. A good liqueur is better. Sherry blends well if the fruit is very ripe and juicy. Peel and slice six hours before serving, pack down in sugar, add the liqueur, and let stand on ice until needed. Peaches cut small, mixed with California grapes, skinned and seeded, also with grape fruit pulp broken small, and drowned in sherry syrup, are surprisingly good. Make the sherry syrup by three parts filling a glass jar with the best lump sugar, pouring on it rather more wine than will cover it, adding the strained juice of a lemon, or orange, a few shreds of yellow peel, and a blade of mace, then setting in sunshine until the sugar dissolves. It should be almost like honey—no other sweetening is needed. A spoonful in after-dinner coffee makes it another beverage—just as a syrup made in the same way from rum, sugar and lemon juice, glorifies afternoon tea.

White grapes halved and seeded mixed with bananas cut small, and orange pulp, well sweetened and topped with whipped cream, either natural or "laced" with sherry, make another easy dessert. Serve in tall footed glasses, set on your finest doilies in your prettiest plates. Lay a flower or a gay candy upon the plate—it adds enormously to the festive effect and very little to the trouble.

A spoonful of rich wine jelly, laid upon any sort of fresh fruit, to my thinking, makes it much better. Cream can be added also—but I do not care for it—indeed do not taste it, nor things creamed. Ripe, juicy cherries, pitted and mixed equally with banana cubes, then sweetened, make a dessert my soul loves to recall. Not caring to eat them I never make ice cream, frozen puddings, *mousses,* sherbets, nor many of the gelatine desserts. Hence I have experimented rather widely in the kingdom of fruits. This book is throughout very largely a record of experience —I hope it may have the more value through being special rather than universal.

Sandwiches: In sandwich making mind your *S's*. That is to say, have your knife sharp, your bread stale, your butter soft.

Moreover the bread must be specially made —fine grained, firm, not crumbly, nor ragged. Cut off crusts for ordinary sandwiches—but if shaping them with cutters let it stay. Then you can cut to the paperthinness requisite—otherwise that is impossible. Work at a roomy table spread with a clean old tablecloth over which put sheets of clean, thick paper. Do your cutting on the papered surface—thus you save either turning your knife edges against a platter or sorely gashing even an old cloth. Keep fancy cutters all together and ready to your hand. Shape one kind of sandwiches all the same—thus you distinguish them easily. Make as many as your paper space will hold, before stamping out any—this saves time and strength. Clear away the fragments from one making, before beginning another sort, thus avoiding possible taints and confusion. Lay your made sandwiches on a platter under a dry cloth with a double damp one on top of it. They will not dry out, and it is much easier than wrapping in oiled paper.

The nearer fillings approach the consistency of soft butter, the better. In making sardine sandwiches, boil the eggs hard, mash the yolks smooth while hot, softening them with either butter or salad dressing —French dressing of course. It is best made with lemon juice and very sharp vinegar for such use. Work into the eggs, the sardines freed of skin and bone after draining well, and mashed as fine as possible. A little of their oil may be added if the flavor is liked. But lemon juice is better. Rub the mixture smooth with the back of a stout wooden spoon, and pack close in a bowl so it shall not harden.

Pimento cheese needs to be softened with French dressing, until like creamed butter. The finer the pimento is ground the better. Spread evenly upon the buttered bread, lay other buttered bread upon it, and pile square. When the pile gets high enough, cut through into triangles or finger shapes, and lay under the damp cloth. Slice Swiss cheese very thin with a sharp knife, season lightly with salt and paprika, and lay between the buttered slices. Lettuce dressed with oil and lemon

juice and lightly sprinkled with Parmesan
cheese makes a refreshing afternoon sandwich. Ham needs to be ground fine—it
must be boiled well of course—seasoned
lightly with made mustard, pepper, and
lemon juice, softened a bit with clear oil
or butter, and spread thin. Tongue must
be treated the same way, else boiled very,
very tender, skinned before slicing, and
sliced paper-thin. Rounds of it inside
shaped sandwiches are likely to surprise
—and please—masculine palates.

For the shaped sandwich—leaf or star,
or heart, or crescent, is the happy home,
generally, of all the fifty-seven varieties
of fancy sandwich fillings, sweet and sour,
mushy and squshy, which make an honest
mouthful of natural flavor, a thing of joy.
Yet this is not saying novelty in sandwiches is undesirable. Contrariwise it is
welcome as summer rain. In witness, here
is a filling from the far Philippines, which
albeit I have not tried it out yet, sounds
to me enticing, and has further the vouch-
ing of a cook most excellent. Grate fine
as much Edam or pineapple cheese as

requisite, season well with paprika, add a few grains of black pepper, wet with sherry to the consistency of cream, and spread between buttered bread. If it is nut bread so much the better. Nut bread is made thus.

Nut Bread for Sandwiches: (Mrs. Petre.) Beat two eggs very light, with a scant teaspoonful salt, half cup sugar, and two cups milk. Sift four cups flour twice with four teaspoonfuls baking powder. Mix with eggs and milk, stir smooth, add one cup nuts finely chopped, let raise for twenty minutes, in a double pan, and bake in a moderately quick oven. Do not try to slice until perfectly cold—better wait till next day, keeping the bread where it will not dry out. Slice very thin, after buttering. Makes sandwiches of special excellence with any sort of good filling.

Pickles, Preserves, Coffee, Tea, Chocolate

Brine for Pickling: Use rain water if possible and regular picking salt—it is coarse and much stronger than cooking salt. Lacking rain water, soften other water by dissolving in it the day beforehand, a pinch of washing soda—this neutralizes largely the mineral contents. Put over the fire in a deep, clean kettle, bring to a boil, put in salt—a pint to the gallon of water is the usual proportion. Boil and skim, add a pinch of saltpeter and tablespoonful of sugar for each pint of salt— the pinches must not be large. Add also six whole cloves for each gallon. Take from fire, let cool, drop in an egg

220

—it should float to show the size of a
quarter of a dollar. Otherwise the brine
needs more salt. Dissolve a pint extra in
as little water as suffices, and add to the
brine, then test again. Put the brine when
cold into a clean, roomy vessel, a keg or
barrel, else a big stone crock. It should
not quite half fill it. Provide a heading
that will float upon it, also a light weight
to keep the heading on the pickles when
put in, and hold them under the brine.
Unless so held the uppermost rot, and spoil
the lot. Mold will gather around the
head in spite of the cloves, but less than
without them. Whenever you put in fresh
pickles, take out the head, wash and scald,
dry, and return to place.

Anything edible will make pickle—still
there are many things better kept out
of the brine. Cabbage and cauliflower
for example do not need it—green tomatoes, onions, and Jerusalem artichokes
are likewise taboo. The artichokes make
good pickle, but it must be made all
at once. Cut anything intended for the
brine with a bit of stalk, and without

bruising the stalk. Cucumbers should be small, and even in size, gherkins about half grown, string beans, three parts grown, crook-neck squash very small and tender, green peppers for mangoes, full grown but not turning, muskmelons for other mangoes three parts grown. Wash clean or wipe with a damp cloth. Cut pickles in early morning, so they may be fresh and crisp. Never put in any wilted bit—thereby you invite decay.

Watermelon rind makes fine pickle. sweet and sour—also citron, queen of all home made preserves. It must be fairly thick, sound and unbruised. The Rattle Snake melon has a good rind for such uses. The finer flavored and thinner-rinded varieties that come to market, are rarely worth cutting up. The cutting up is a bit tedious. The rind must be cut in strips rather more than an inch wide and three to five inches long, then trimmed on each side, free of green outer skin, and all trace of the soft inside. There will remain less than half an inch thickness of firm pale green tissue with potentialities of delight—if you know how to bring them out.

Firm clingstone peaches not fully ripe, can be put in the brine—they had better, however, be pickled without it. For whatever is put in, and saved by salt, must be freed of the salt by long soaking before it is fit to eat. The soaking process is the same for everything—take from brine, wash clean in tepid water, put to soak in cold water with something on top to hold the pickles down. Change water twice the first day, afterward every day, until it has not the least salt taste.

You can make pickle by soaking in brine three days, then washing clean, putting over the fire in clear water, bringing to scalding heat, then pouring off the water, covering with vinegar, and bringing just to a boil. Drain away this vinegar, which has served its turn, pack down the pickles in a jar, seasoning them well with mixed spices, whole, not in powder, covering with fresh, hot vinegar, letting cool uncovered, then tieing down, and keep dark and cool.

Watermelon Rind Pickle: Scald the

soaked rind in strong ginger tea, let stand two minutes barely simmering, then skim out, lay in another kettle, putting in equal quantities of cloves, mace, alspice, and cinnamon, half as much grated nutmeg, the same of whole pepper corns, several pods of Cayenne pepper, white mustard and celery seed, covering with cider vinegar, the only sort that will keep pickles well, bringing just to the boil, then putting down hot in jars, tying down after cooling, and setting in a dark, cool, airy place.

For sweet pickle, prepare and season, then to each pint of vinegar put one and a half pounds of sugar, boil together one minute, stirring well, and skimming clean, then pour over rind and spices, keep hot for ten minutes without boiling, then put into jars. If wanted only a little sweet, use but half a pound of sugar.

Mangoes: Either green peppers or young melons will serve as a foundation —epicures rather preferring the peppers. After making thoroughly fresh, cut out the stems from the peppers, removing and throwing away the seed but saving the stems. Cut a section from the side of each melon, and remove everything inside. Fit back stems, sections, etc., then pack in a kettle in layers with fresh grape leaves between, add a bit of alum as big as the thumb's end, cover all with strong, cold vinegar, bring to a boil, and simmer gently for twenty minutes. Let stand in vinegar two or three days, throwing away the leaves. Take out, rinse and drain. To stuff four dozen, bruise, soak, cut small and dry, half a pound of race ginger, add half a pint each black and white mustard seed, mace, allspice, Turmeric, black pepper, each half an ounce, beat all together to a rather fine powder, add a dash of garlic, and mix smooth in half a cup of salad oil. Chop very fine a small head of firm but tender cabbage, three fine hearts of celery, half a dozen small pickled cucumbers, half a pint small onions, a large, sweet red pepper, finely shredded, add a teaspoonful sugar, a tablespoonful of brandy, or dry sherry, the mixed spices, work all well together, stuff the mangoes neatly, sew up with soft thread or tie about with very narrow tape, pack down in stone jars, cover with the best cold vinegar, pour a film of salad oil on top, tie down and let stand two months. If wanted sweetish, add moist sugar to the vinegar, a pound to the gallon. Mangoes are for men in the general—and men like things hot and sour.

Walnut Pickle: Gather white walnuts in June—they must be tender enough to cut with the finger nail. Wash, drain and pack down in jars smothered in salt. Let stand a fortnight, drain off the resultant brine then, scald the nuts in strong vinegar, let stand hot, but not boiling, for twenty minutes, then drain, and pack in jars, putting between the layers, a mixture of cloves, alspice, black and red pepper, in equal quantity, with half as much mace, nutmeg, cinnamon and ginger. Strew in a very little salt, and a little more sugar. Mix mustard and celery seed in a cup of salad oil, and add to the jars, after the nuts are in. Scald strong cider vinegar, skim clean, let cool, pour over the prepared nuts, film with oil on top. Leave open for two days—if the vinegar

sinks through absorption, fill up the jars.
Paste paper over mouths, tie down securely, and set in a cool place until next
year. It takes twelve months for pickled
walnuts fully to ''find themselves.''

Preserving Fruit: Peaches, pears,
plums, or cherries, the process is much the
same. Use the finest fruit, ripe but not
over-ripe. There is no greater waste of
strength, time, and sugar, than in preserving tasteless, inferior fruit. Pare peaches
and drop instantly in water to save discoloration. Do the same with pears, pit
cherries, saving the juice. Wash and
prick plums if large—if small, merely
wash and drain. Halve clear stone peaches
but put in a few seeds for the flavor.
Leave cling-stones on the seed, unless very
large, else saw them in three, across the
stones. They make less handsome preserves thus sawn but of finer flavor.
Weigh, take pound for pound of sugar,
with a pound over for the kettle. Very
acid fruit, cherries or gooseberries, will
require six pounds of sugar to four of
fruit. Pack pears and peaches after

paring in the sugar over night. Drain off the syrup at morning, put the fruit in the kettle, cover with strained ginger tea, and simmer for ten minutes. Meantime cook the sugar and fruit juice in another kettle. Drop the fruit hot in the boiling syrup, set the kettle in a hot oven, and let it cook there until the preserves are done—the fruit clear, and the syrup thick. If it is not rich enough, skim out the fruit, and reduce the syrup by rapid boiling, then pour over the hot fruit in jars.

It is only by cooking thus in ginger tea, or plain water, pear and quince preserves can be made soft. Quinces do not need to stand overnight in sugar—rather heat the sugar, and put it in the liquid they have been boiled in, after skimming out the fruit. It should be cooked without sugar till a fork easily pierces it, but not until it begins to rag.

Put cherry juice and sugar over the fire, adding a little water if juice is scant, boil up, stirring well and skimming clean, then put in the fruit, and let it simmer ten minutes, and finish by setting the kettle in the oven till the preserves are rich and thick.

Fancy peach preserves require white, juicy fruit cut up, but not too thin. Let it stand in sugar overnight—drain off syrup in morning, boil, skim clean, then drop in fruit a handful at a time, and cook till clear. Skim out, put in more, lay cooked fruit on platters, and set under glass in sun. Sun all day. Next day boil syrup a little more, drop in fruit, heat through, then put all in clear glass jars, and set for ten days in hot sunshine, covered close. The fruit should be a rich translucent pink, the syrup as rich as honey, and a little lighter pink. These are much handsomer than the gingered peaches but not so good. Ginger tea in syrup makes it always darker.

Plums require nothing extra in the way of flavoring. Make a very thick syrup of the sugar and a little water, skim clean, drop in the pricked plums, and cook gently till clear. Skim out, reduce the syrup by further boiling and pour it over the fruit, packed in jars. By oven-cooking after a good boil up, there is so little occasion for stirring, the plums are left almost entirely whole.

Ginger Pears: (Leslie Fox.) Four pounds pears peeled and cut small, four pounds granulated sugar, juice of four lemons, and the grated peel of two, two ounces preserved ginger cut very fine. Cook all together over a slow fire until thick and rich—it should make a firm jelly. Put away in glass with brandy paper on top the same as other preserves.

Tutti Frutti: (Mrs. J. R. Oldham.) Begin by getting a big wide-mouthed jar, either thoroughly glazed earthenware, or thick, dark glass. Wash well, fill with hot water, add a half-pound washing soda, and let stand a day. Empty, rinse three times, and wipe dry. Thus you make end to potential molds and microbes. Do this in early spring. Put into the jar, a quart of good brandy and a tablespoonful of mixed spices—any your taste approves, also a little finely shredded yellow peel of lemons and oranges. Wash well and hull a quart of fine ripe strawberries, add them with their own weight in sugar to the brandy, let stand till raspberries and cherries are ripe, then put in a quart of each, along with their weight in sugar. Do this with all fruit as it comes in season—forced fruit, or that shipped long distances has not enough flavor. Add grapes, halved and seeded, gooseberries, nibbed and washed, blackberries, peaches pared and quartered. Currants are best left out, but by no means slight plums. The big meaty sorts are best. Add as much sugar as fruit, and from time to time more brandy—there must be always enough to stand well above the fruit. Add spices also as the jar grows, and if almond flavor is approved, kernels of all the stone fruit, well blanched. Lay on a saucer or small plate, when the jar is full, to hold the fruit well under the liquor. Tie down, and leave standing for three months. Fine for almost any use—especially to sauce mild puddings.

Green Tomato Preserves: Take medium size tomatoes, smooth, even, meaty,

just on the point of turning but still green.
Pare very carefully with a sharp knife.
Cut out eyes, taking care not to cut into
a seed cavity. Weigh—to four pounds
fruit take six of sugar. Lay the peeled
tomatoes in clear lime water for an hour,
take out, rinse, and simmer for ten minutes in strained ginger tea. Make a syrup
in another kettle, putting half a cup water
to the pound of sugar. Skim clean, put
in the tomatoes, add the strained juice of
lemons—three for a large kettle full, and
simmer for two hours, until the fruit is
clear. Cut the lemon rind in strips, boil
tender in strong salt water, then boil fresh
in clear water, and add to the syrup.
Simmer all together for another hour, then
skim out the fruit, boil the syrup to the
thickness of honey, and pour over the tomatoes after putting them in jars. It
ought to be very clear, and the tomatoes
a pale, clear green. Among the handsom-
est of all preserves, also the most delicious,
once you get the hang of making them.
Ripe yellow tomatoes are preserved the
same way, except that they are scalded for

peeling, and hardened by dropping in alum water after their lime-water bath. The same process applied to watermelon rind after it is freshened makes citron.

Brandy Peaches and Pears: These can be made without cooking. Choose ripe, perfect fruit, pare, stick three cloves in each, weigh, take pound for pound of sugar with one over for the jar. Pack down in a large jar, putting spices between, and filling sugar into every crevice. Crowd in every bit possible, then pour on enough whiskey to stand an inch above the fruit. Let stand—in twenty four hours more whiskey will be needed. Fill up, sprinkle a few more whole cloves on top, also two small pods of Cayenne pepper, and half a dozen pepper corns. Tie down and keep cool. Fit for use in a fortnight, and of fine keeping quality. The same treatment with vinegar in place of whiskey makes very good sweet pickle.

Another way, is to pack the fruit in sugar over night, drain off the juice at morning, boil and skim it, and pour back upon the fruit. Repeat twice—the third time put everything in the kettle, cook till a fork will pierce the fruit, then pack in jars, adding spices to taste, and one fourth as much whiskey as there is fruit and syrup. This likewise can be turned into very rich sweet pickle, by using vinegar instead of whiskey, putting it with the syrup at first boiling, sticking cloves in the fruit, and adding spices to taste.

Throw stemmed and washed cherries, unpitted, into thick syrup made of their weight in sugar with half a cup water to the pound. Let boil, set in oven for half an hour, take up, add spices, and either brandy or vinegar, in the proportion of one to three. Let stand uncovered to cool, put in jars, cover with brandy paper, tie down and keep dark and cool.

Tea: *Coffee*: *Chocolate*: My tea-making is unorthodox, but people like to drink the brew. Bring fresh water to a bubbling boil in a clean, wide kettle, throw in the tea—a tablespoonful to the gallon of water, let boil just one minute, then strain from the leaves into a pot that has stood for five minutes full of freshly boiled water, and that is instantly wrapped about with a thick napkin, so it shall not cool. Serve in tall glasses with rum and lemon, or with sherry syrup, flavored with lemon, add a Maraschino cherry or so, or a tiny bit of ginger-flavored citron. This for the unorthodox. Those who are orthodox can have cream either whipped or plain, with rock candy crystals instead of sugar.

Coffee to be absolutely perfect should never get cold betwixt the beginning of roasting and the end of drinking. Since that is out of the question save to Grand Turks and faddists, mere mortals must make shift with coffee freshly ground, put in a very clean pot, with the least suspicion of salt—about six fine grains to the cupful, fresh cold water, in the proportion of three cupfuls to two heaping spoonfuls of ground coffee, then the pot set where it will take twenty minutes to boil, and so carefully watched it can not possibly boil over. Boiling over ruins it—makes it flat, bitter, aroma-less. So does long boiling —one minute, no more, is the longest boiling time. Quick boiling is as bad—the

water has not time to extract the real good-
ness of the coffee. Let stand five minutes
to clear, keeping hot. Those who drink
coffee half milk may like it stronger—a
cupful of water to the heaping spoonful
of coffee. I do not thus abuse one of the
crowning mercies, so make my coffee the
strength I like to drink it. Reducing with
boiling water spoils the taste for me. So
does pouring into another pot—my silver
pot is used only upon occasions when cere-
mony must outweigh hospitality. In very
cold weather hot water may well warm cups
both for tea and coffee. Standing on the
grounds does not spoil the flavor of coffee
as it does tea.

Coffee from the original pot is quite another affair from the same thing shifted.
I am firmly of opinion that many a pat-
ent coffee-maker has gone on to success
through the fact that cups were filled di-
rectly from the urn. I always feel that
I taste my coffee mostly with my nose—
nothing refreshes me like the clean, keen
fragrance of it—especially after broken
rest. It is idle to talk as so many

authorities do, of using "Java and Mocha blended." All the real Java and Mocha in the world is snapped up, long before it filters down to the average level. Back in the Dark Ages of my childhood, I knew experimentally real Java—we got it by the sack-full straight from New Orleans—and called the Rio coffee used by many of our neighbors "Seed tick coffee," imagining its flavor was like the smell of those pests. Nowadays, Rio coffee has pretty well the whole world for its parish. Wherefore the best one can do, is to get it sound, well roasted, and as fresh as may be. Much as I love and practice home preparation, I am willing to let the Trust or who will, roast my coffee. Roasting is parlous work, hot, tedious, and tiresome, also mighty apt to result in scorching if not burning. One last caution—never meddle with the salt unless sure your hand is light, your memory so trustworthy you will not put it in twice.

Chocolate spells milk, and cream, and trouble, hence I make it only on occasions of high state. Yet—I am said to make it well. Perhaps the secret lies in the brandy—a scant teaspoonful for each cake of chocolate grated. Put in a bowl after grating, add the brandy, stir about, then add enough hot water to dissolve smoothly, and stir into a quart of rich milk, just brought to a boil. Add six lumps of sugar, stir till dissolved, pour into your pot, which must have held boiling water for five minutes previously, and serve in heated cups, with or without whipped cream on top. There is no taste of the brandy— it appears merely to give a smoothness to the blending. If the chocolate is too rich, half-fill cups with boiling water, then pour in the chocolate. There are brands of chocolate which can be made wholly of water—they will serve at a pinch, but are not to be named with the real thing. Cocoa I have never made, therefore say nothing about its making. Like Harry Percy's wife, in cooking at least, I "never tell that which I do not know."

When the Orchards "Hit"

When the peach orchard "hit" it meant
joy to the plantation. Peaches had so
many charms—and there were so many
ways of stretching the charms on through
winter scarcity. Peach drying was in a
sort, a festival, especially if there were a
kiln, which made one independent of the
weather. It took many hands wielding
many sharp knives in fair fruit to keep
a kiln of fair size running regularly. This
though it were no more than a thing of
flat stones and clean clay mud, with paper
laid over the mud, and renewed periodically. There was a shed roof, over the kiln,
which sat commonly in the edge of the
orchard. Black Daddy tended the firing

—with a couple of active lads to cut and fetch wood, what time they were not fetching in great baskets of peaches.

Yellow peaches, not too ripe but full flavored, made the lightest and sweetest dried fruit. And clingstones were ever so much better for drying than the clear-seed sorts. Some folk took off the peach fuzz with lye —they did not, I think, save trouble thereby, and certainly lost somewhat in the flavor of their fruit. Mammy was a past mistress of cutting "cups." That is to say, half-peaches, with only the seed deftly removed. She sat with the biggest bread tray upon her well cushioned knees, in the midst of the peelers, who as they peeled, dropped their peaches into the tray.

When it over-ran with cups, somebody slimmer and suppler, took it away, and spread the cut fruit, just touching, all over the hot kiln. It must not be too hot —just so you couldn't bear the back of your hand to it was about right. Daddy kept the temperature even, by thrusting into the flues underneath it, long sticks of green wood, kindled well at the flue-mouths.

Cups shrank mightily in a little while—you could push of an early trayful till it would no more than cover space the size of a big dish, long before dinner time—in other words twelve o'clock—drying was in full blast by seven. With fruit in gluts, and dropping fast, the kiln was supplemented by scaffolds. Clean planks laid upon trestles, and set in full sunshine, gave excellent accounts of themselves. This of course if the sun shone steadily—in showery weather scaffold-drying was no end of trouble. Weather permitting, it made—it still makes—the finest and most flavorous dried fruit ever eaten.

The black people chose clear-seed peaches for their individual drying. They made merry over splitting the fruit, and placing it, sitting out in front of their cabins in the moonshine, or by torch-light. Washing was all they gave the peach outsides—a little thing like a fuzzy rind their palates did not object to. It was just as well, since clear-seed fruit, peeled, shrinks unconscionably—to small scrawny knots, inclined to be sticky—though it is but just to add, that in cooking, it comes back to almost its original succulence. When the peach-cutting was done, there was commonly a watermelon feast. Especially at Mammy's house—Daddy's watermelons were famed throughout the county. He gave seed of them sparingly, and if the truth must be told, rather grudgingly—but nobody ever brought melons to quite his pitch of perfection. Possibly because he planted for the most part, beside rotting stumps in the new ground, where the earth had to be kept light and clean for tobacco, and where the vines got somewhat of shade, and the roots fed fat upon the richness of virgin soil.

It took eight bushels of ripe fruit, to make one of dry—this when the peaches were big and fleshy. Small, seedy sorts demanded ten bushels for one. Unpeeled, the ratio fell to seven for one. But there was seldom any lack of fruit—beside the orchard, there were trees up and down all the static fence rows—the corner of a worm fence furnishing an ideal seat. Further, every field boasted trees, self-planted, sprung from chance seed vagrantly cast. These volunteer trees often had the very best fruit—perhaps because only peaches of superior excellence had been worth carrying a-field. Tilth also helped—the field trees bent and often broke under their fruity burdens. It was only when late frosts made half or three parts of the young fruit drop, that we knew how fine and beautiful these field peaches could be. Our trees, being all seedlings, were in a degree, immortelles. Branches, even trunks might bend and break, but the seminal roots sent up new shoots next season, which in another year, bore fruit scantily. Still, these renewals never gave quite such perfect fruit as grew upon vigorous young trees, just come to full bearing.

Here or there a plantation owner like my starch and stately grandfather, turned surplus peaches into brandy. In that happy time excise was—only a word in the dictionary, so the yield of certain trees, very free-bearing, of small, deep, red, clearseed fruit, was allowed to get dead-ripe on the trees, then mashed to a pulp in the cider trough, and put into stands to ferment, then duly distilled. Barrelled, after two years in the lumber house, it was racked into clean barrels, and some part of it converted into "peach and honey," the favorite gentleman's tipple. Strained honey was mixed with the brandy in varying proportions—the amount depending somewhat upon individual tastes. Some used one measure of honey to three of brandy, others put one to two, still others, half and half, qualifying the sweetness by adding neat brandy at the time of drinking. Peach and honey was kept properly in stone jugs or in demijohns, improved mightily with age, and was, at its best, to the last degree insidious. Newly mixed it was heady, but after a year or more, as smooth as oil, and as mellow. The honey had something to do with final excellence. That which the bees gathered from wild raspberries in flower, being very clear, light-colored and fine-flavored, was in especial request.

I think these peaches of the brandy orchards traced back to those the Indians,

Creeks, Choctaws, and Cherokees, planted in the mountain valleys of Georgia, North Carolina, Tennessee, and Virginia. They got the seed from early Spaniard voyagers to Florida. There was indeed a special Indian peach, as dark-skinned as its namesake, blood-red inside and out, very sweet and full of juice, if permitted to ripen fully—but as ill-tasting almost as a green persimmon, if unripe. There were clearstone and clingstone sorts, and one tree differed from another in glory of flavor, even as one star. That was the charm of our seedlings—which had further a distinction of flavor no commercial fruit ever yet owned.

August peaches were **for** drying—in September, early, came the Heaths, for preserves, brandy fruit, and so on. October peaches, nearly all clear-seed, made the finest peach butter. Understand, in those days, canning, known as "hermetic sealing," was still a laboratory process. I wonder if anybody else recalls, as I do, the first editions of fruit cans? They were of tin, tall and straight, with a flaring upstanding tin ruffle around the tops. The ruffle was for holding the sealing wax, into which the edge of the tin top was thrust. They did not last long—pretty soon, there were cans of the present shape— but sealing them with wax was hard work, likewise uncertain. Women everywhere should rise and call blessed he who invented the self-sealing jar.

Return we to our peach butter. It began in cider—the cider from fall apples, very rich and sweet. To boil it down properly required a battery of brass kettles swung over a log fire in the yard, the same as at drying up lard time. Naturally brass kettles were at a premium—but luckily everybody did not make peach butter, so it was no strain upon neighborly comity to borrow of such. It took more than half a day to boil down the cider properly—kettles were filled up constantly as there was room. By and by, when the contents became almost syrup, peaches went in—preferably the late, soft, white ones, dead ripe, very juicy, and nearly as sweet as sugar. After the kettles were full of them, peeled and halved, of course, the boiling went on until the fruit was mushy. Constant stirring helped to make it so. Fresh peaches were added twice, and cooked down until the paddle stood upright in the middle of the kettle. Then came the spicing—putting in cloves, mace, bruised ginger, and alspice—sparingly, but enough to flavor delicately. If the white peaches ran short, there might be a supplemental butter-making when the Red Octobers came in, at the very last of the month. They were big and handsome, oval, with the richest crimson cheeks, but nothing like so sweet as the white ones. So sugar, or honey, was added scantly, at the end of the boiling down. If it had been put in earlier, it would have added to the danger of burning.

A six-gallon crock of peach butter was no mean household asset—indeed it ranked next to the crock of blackberry jam. It was good as a sauce, or lightly sweetened, to spread on crust. As a filling for roly-polys it had but one superior—namely dried peaches properly stewed.

Proper stewing meant washing a quart of dry fruit in two waters, soaking overnight, then putting over the fire in the soaking water, covering with a plate to hold the fruit down, and simmering at the least five hours, filling up the kettle from time to time, and adding after the fruit was soft a pound of sugar. Then at the very last spices to taste went in. If the fruit were to be eaten along with meat, as a relish, a cupful of vinegar was added after the sugar. This made it a near approach to the finest sweet pickle. But as Mammy said often: "Dried peaches wus good ernough fer anybody—dest by dee sefs, dry so."

Apple drying commonly came a little before peach. Horse apples, the best and plentiest, ripened in the beginning of August. They were kiln-dried, or scaffold-dried, and much less tedious than peaches since they were sliced thin. When they got very mellow, drying ceased—commonly everybody had plenty by that time—and the making of apple butter began. It differed little from peach butter in the making, though mightily in taste—being of a less piquant flavor. Cider, newly run was essential to any sort of butter—hence the beating was done before breakfast. Cider mills were not—but cider troughs abounded. They were dug from huge poplar logs, squared outside with the broad axe, and adzed within to a smooth finish. Apples well washed, were beaten in them with round headed wooden pestles, and pressed in slat presses, the pomace laid on clean straw, after the manner of cider pressing in English orchards. The first runnings, somewhat muddy, were best for boiling down, but the clear last runnings drank divinely—especially after keeping until there was just the trace of sparkle to them.

Winter cider was commonly allowed to get hard. So was that meant for distilling —apple brandy was only second to peach. But a barrel or keg, would be kept sweet for women, children, and ministers—either by smoking the inside of a clean barrel well with sulphur before putting in the cider, or by hanging inside a barrel nearly full, a thin muslin bag full of white mustard seed. Cider from russets and pear apples had a peculiar excellence, so was kept for Christmas and other high days.

Pear cider—perry—we knew only in books. Not through lack of pears but inclination to make it. Pears were dried the same as other fruit, but commonly packed down after drying in sugar. Thus they were esteemed nearly as good as peach chips, or even peach leather.

Peach chips were sliced thin, packed down in their own weight of sugar and let stand twenty-four hours to toughen. Then the syrup was drained from them, boiled, skimmed clean, spiced with mace and lemon peel, and the slices dropped into it a few at a time and cooked until sweet through. Then they were skimmed out, spread on dishes well sprinkled with sugar, dredged with more sugar, set under glass in sunshine and turned daily until dry. They were delicious, and served as other confections—passed around with nuts and wine, or eaten instead of candy.

So were cherries, dried in exactly the

same manner, after pitting. When dried without sugar they were used for cooking. So also were tomato figs. Yellow tomatoes, smooth and even were best—but red ones answered—the meatier the better. After scalding, peeling, soaking an hour in clear lime-water to harden, they were rinsed clean, then dropped in thick boiling syrup, a few at a time, simmered an hour, then skimmed out, drained, sugared and dried under glass in the sun, or failing sunshine, upon dishes in a very slow oven. Full-dry, they were packed down in powdered sugar, in glass jars kept tightly closed. Unless thus kept they had a knack of turning sticky—which defeated the purpose of their creation.

Peach leather may not appeal to this day of many sweets—but it was good indeed back in the spare elder time. To make it the very ripest, softest peaches were peeled, and mashed smooth, working quickly so the pulp might not color too deeply, then spread an inch thick upon large dishes or even clean boards, and dried slowly in sunshine or the oven.

After it was full-dry, came the cutting into inch-strips. This took a very sharp knife and a steady hand. Then the strips were coiled edgewise into flat rounds, with sugar between the rounds of the coils, which had to be packed down in more sugar and kept close, to save them from dampness, which meant ruin.

If you had a fond and extravagant grandmother, you were almost sure to have also a clove apple. That is to say, a fine firm winter apple, stuck as full of cloves as it could hold, then allowed to dry very, very slowly, in air neither hot nor cold. The cloves banished decay—their fragrance joined to the fruity scent of the apple, certainly set off things kept in the drawer with the apple. The applemakers justified their extravagance—cloves cost money, then as now—by asserting a belief in clove apples as sovereign against mildew or moths—which may have had a color of reason.

The quince tree is the clown of the orchard, growing twisted and writhing, as though hating a straight line. Notwith-

standing, its fruit, and the uses thereof, set
the hall mark of housewifery. Especially
in the matter of jelly-making and marmalade. Further a quince pudding is in the
nature of an experience—so few have ever
heard of it, so much fewer made or tasted
it. The making requires very ripe quinces
—begin by scrubbing them clean of fuzz,
then set them in a deep pan, cover, after
adding a tablespoonful of water, and bake
slowly until very soft. Scrape out the
pulp, throw away cores and skin. To a
pint of pulp take four eggs, beat the yolks
light with three cups of sugar and a cup of
creamed butter, add the quince pulp, a little mace broken small or grated nutmeg,
then half a cup of cream, and the egg-
whites beaten stiff. Bake in a deep pan,
and serve hot with hard or wine sauce.

Here are some fine points of jelly-making learned in that long ago. To make the
finest, clearest jelly, cook but little at a
time. A large kettleful will never have
the color and brightness of two or three
glasses. Never undertake to make jelly
of inferior fruit—that which is unripe or

over-ripe, or has begun to sour. Wash clean, and drain—paring is not only waste work, but in a measure lessens flavor. Put a little water with the fruit when you begin cooking it—cook rather slowly so there shall be no scorching, and drain out rather than press out the juice. Draining is much freer if the fruit is spread thin, rather than dumped compactly in a bag. Double cheese cloth sewed fast over stout wire, and laid on top of a wide bowl, makes a fine jelly drainer—one cheap enough to be thrown away when discolored. A discolored bag, by the way, makes jelly a bit darker. If there is no pressure flannel is not required.

Plenty as fruit was with us, Mammy made jelly and marmalade from the same quinces. They were well washed, peeled, quartered and the cores removed, then the quarters boiled until soft in water to half-cover them, skimmed out, mashed smooth with their own weight of sugar, and spices to taste, then cooked very slowly until the spoon stood upright in the mass, after which it went into glass jars, and had a brandy paper laid duly on top.

Cores and paring were boiled to rags in water to fully cover them, then strained out, the water strained again, and added to that in which the fruit had boiled. Sugar was added—a pound to the pint of juice. But first the juice was brought to a boil, and skimmed very clean. The sugar, heated without scorching, went in, and cooking continued until the drop on the tip of the spoon jellied as it fell. Mammy hated jelly that ran—it must cut like butter to reach her standard. Occasionally she flavored it with ginger—boiling the bruised root with the cores—but only occasionally, as ginger would make the jelly darker. Occasionally also she cooked apples, usually fall pippins, with the quinces, thus increasing the bulk of both jelly and marmalade, with hardly a sensible diminution of flavor.

All here written applies equally to every sort of fruit jelly—apple, peach, currant, the whole family of berries. Mammy never knew it, but I myself have found the oven at half-heat a very present help in jelly-making. Fruit well prepared, and put into a stone or agate vessel, covered and baked gently for a time proportionate to its bulk, yields all its juice, and it seems to me clearer juice, than when stewed in the time-honored brass kettle. Hot sugar helps to jellying quickly—and the more haste there, the lighter and brighter the result. Gelatin in fruit jellies I never use —it increases the product sensibly, but that is more than offset by the decrease in quality.

Upon Occasions

It was no trouble at all to make occasions. Indeed, the greatest of them, weddings, really made themselves. A wedding made imperative an infare—that is to say, if the high contracting parties had parental approval. Maybe I had better explain that infare meant the bride's going home—to her new house, or at least her new family. This etymologically—the root is the Saxon *faran,* to go, whence come wayfaring, faring forth and so on. All this I am setting forth not in pedantry, but because so many folk had stared blankly upon hearing the word—which was to me as familiar as word could be. In application it had a wide latitude. Commonly the groom or his famly gave the infare, but often enough some generous and well-to-do friend, or kinsman, pre-empted the privilege. Wherever held, it was an occasion of keen and jealous rivalry—those in charge being doubly bent on making the faring in more splendid than the wedding feast. Naturally that put the wedding folk on their mettle. Another factor inciting to extra effort was—the bundles. All guests were expected to take home with them generous bundles of wedding cake in all its varieties. I recall once hearing a famous cake baker sigh relief as she frosted the hundredth snow ball, and said: "Now we are sure to have enough left for the bundles—they are such a help."

But baking cakes, and cooking in general, though important, were not the main things. Setting the table, so it should outshine all other wedding tables gave most concern. To this end all the resources of the family, and its friends for a radius of ten miles, were available—glass, silver, china, linen, even cook pots and ovens at

need. Also and further it was a slight of
the keenest, if you were known as a fine
cake maker, not to be asked to help. A past
mistress of paper cutting was likewise in
request. Cut papers and evergreens were
the great reliances in decoration. They
made a brave showing by candlelight. Oil
lamps were few, kerosene undiscovered,
and either lard oil, or whale oil, all too
often smelled to heaven, to say nothing of
smoking upon the least provocation. So a
lamp, if there were one, sat in state within
the parlor. The long table got its light
from candelabra—which as often as not
were homemade. The base was three
graduated blocks of wood, nailed to form
a sort of pyramid, with a hole bored in the
middle to receive a stout round upright,
two inches across. It stood a foot high,
and held up cross-arms three feet across,
with a tin candlesocket upon each end.
Another socket was set where the arms
crossed—thus each candelabra was of five-
candle power. Set a-row down the middle
of the table, with single candles in tall
brass sticks interspersed, they gave a fine

soft illumination. Often they were supplemented with candelabra of bronze or brass, tricked out with tinkly pendant prisms. Such household gauds were commonly concentrated at the spot where the bride and her maids would stand. They were more elegant, of course, than the made candle-holders—but not to my thinking a whit the handsomer—after the papercutters had done their work.

Their work was turning white paper into fringe and lace. Fringed strips wound all over and about, hid the foundation wood. Paper tulips, deftly fashioned, held the tin rings in ambush—with clusters of lacy leaves pendant below. Sometimes a paper rose tipped each arm-end—sometimes also, there were pendant sprays of pea-shaped blossoms. How they were made, with nothing beyond scissors, pen-knives for crimping, and the palm of the hand for mold, I confess I do not understand—but I know they were marvels. The marvels required a special knack, of course—also much time and patience. Wherefore those who had it, exercised it in scraps of leisure as paper came to hand, laying away the results against the next wedding even though none were imminent. Leaves and the round lace-edged pieces to go under cakes, it was easy thus to keep. Flowers, roses, tulips and so on, had a trick of losing shape—besides, although so showy, they were really much easier to make.

It took nice contrivance to make table-room—but double thicknesses of damask falling to the floor either side hid all roughness in the foundation. Shape depended much upon the size of the supper-room—if it were but an inclosed piazza, straight length was imperative. But in a big square or parallelogram, one could easily achieve a capital *H*—or else a letter *Z*. *Z* was rather a favorite in that it required less heavy decoration, yet gave almost as much space. A heart-cake for either tip, a stack at each acute angle, with the bride's cake midway the stem, flanked either hand by bowls of syllabub and boiled custard, made a fine showing. A letter *H* demanded four heartcakes—one for each end, also four stacks, and crowded the bride and her party along the joining bar.

Heart-cakes were imperative to any wedding of degree. Local tinsmiths made the moulds for them—they were deeply cleft, and not strictly classic of outline. But, well and truly baked, frosted a glistening white, then latticed and fringed with more frosting, dribbled on delicately from the point of a tube, they were surely good to look at. If the bride's cake were white all through, the heart-pans were usually filled with gold-cake batter—thus white and yolk of eggs had equal honor. More commonly though, the most part of wedding cake was pound cake in the beginning—the richer the better. Baked in deep round-bottomed, handleless coffee cups, and iced, it made the helpful snow balls. Baked in square pans, rather shallow, cut into bars, crisped, frosted and piled cob-house fashion, it made pens. Sliced crosswise and interlaid with jelly it became jelly cake. To supplement it, there were marble cake, spice cake, plum cake, ever so many more cakes—but they were—only supplements.

Stacks were either round or square,

baked in pans of graduated size, set one on the other after cooling thoroughly, then frosted and re-frosted till they had a polar suggestion. If round there was commonly a hole running down the middle, into this was fitted a wide mouthed but small glass bottle, to hold the stems of the evergreen plume topping the stack. Here or there in the plume, shone a paper rose or star-flower—in the wreath of evergreen laid about the base, were tulips, lilies, and bigger roses, all made of paper. Occasionally trailing myrtle, well washed and dried, was put about the components of the stacks just before they were set in place. If the heart-cakes had missed being latticed, they likewise were myrtle-wreathed. The bride's cake was left dead-white, but it always stood on something footed, and had a wreath of evergreen and paper flowers, laid upon a lace-cut paper about the foot.

Baking it was an art. So many things had to go in it—the darning needle, thimble, picayune, ring, and button. The makers would have scorned utterly the modern subterfuge of baking plain, and thrusting in the portents of fate before frosting. They mixed the batter a trifle stiff, washed and scoured everything, shut eyes, dropped them, and stirred them well about. Thus nobody had the least idea where they finally landed—so the cutting was bound to be strictly fair. It made much fun—the bride herself cut the first slice—hoping it might hold the picayune, and thus symbolize good fortune. The ring presaged the next bride or groom, the darning needle single blessedness to the end, the thimble, many to sew for, or feed, the button, fickleness or disappointment. After the bridal party had done cutting, other young folk tempted fate. Bride's cake was not for eating—instead, fragments of it, duly wrapped and put under the pillow, were thought to make whatever the sleeper dreamed come true. Especially if the dream included a sweetheart, actual or potential. The dreams were supposed to be truly related next day at the infare—but I question if they always were. Perhaps the magic worked—and in this wise—the person dreamed of took on so new a significance, the difference was quickly felt. But this is a cook book—with reminiscent attachments, not a treatise on psychology.

The table held only the kickshaws—cakes, candy, nuts, syllabub and custard. Wide handsome plates piled high with tempting sliced cake sat up and down the length of it, with glass dishes of gay candies in between. In cold weather wine jelly often took the place of syllabub. There were neither napkins nor service plates—all such things came from the side table, the plates laden with turkey, ham, fried chicken, or broiled, and some sort of jelly or relish. One ate standing, with her escort doing yeoman service as waiter, until her appetite was fully appeased. Hot biscuit, hot egg bread, and light bread —salt rising, freshly sliced—were passed about by deft black servitors. The side tables were under charge of family friends, each specially skilled in helping and serving. Carving, of course, had been done before hand. Occasionally, very occasionally, where a wedding throng ran well into the hundreds, there was barbecue in addition to other meat. In that case it was cut up outside, and sent in upon huge platters. But it was more a feature of infares, held commonly by daylight, than of wedding suppers.

Wedding salad is set forth in its proper chapter, but not the turkey hash that was to some minds the best of all the good eating. It was served for breakfast— there was always a crowd of kinfolk and faraway friends to stay all night—sleeping on pallets all over the floors, even those of parlor or ballroom, after they were deserted. The hash was made from all the left-over turkey—where a dozen birds have been roasted the leavings will be plenty. To it was added the whole array of giblets, cooked the day before, and cut small while still warm. They made heaps of rich gravy to add to that in the turkey pots—no real wedding ever contented itself with cooking solely on a range. Pots, big ones, set beside a log fire out of doors, with a little water in the bottom, and coals underneath and on the lids, turned out turkeys beautifully browned, tender and flavorous, to say nothing of the gravy. It set off the hash as nothing else could—but such setting off was not badly needed. Hash with hot biscuit, strong clear coffee, hot egg bread, and thin-sliced ham, made a breakfast one could depend on, even with a long drive cross-country in prospect.

Harking back to the supper table—syllabub, as nearly as I recall, was made of thick cream lightly reinforced with stiffly beaten white of egg—one egg-white to each pint—sweetened, well flavored with sherry or Madeira wine, then whipped very stiff, and piled in a big bowl, also in goblets to set about the bowl, just as snow balls were set a-row about the stacks and the bride's cake. Flecks of crimson jelly were dropped on the white cream—occasionally, there were crumbled cake, and cut up fruit underneath. Thus it approximated the trifle of the cook books. It had just one drawback—you could not eat it slowly—it went almost to nothing at the agitation of the spoon.

Far otherwise boiled custard—which was much higher in favor, being easier made, and quite as showy. For it you beat very light the yolks of twelve eggs with four cups white sugar, added them to a gallon of milk, and a quart of cream, in a brass kettle over the fire, stirred the mixture steadily, watching it close to remove it just as it was on the point of boiling, let it cool, then flavored it well, with either whiskey, brandy, or sweet wine. Meantime the egg-whites beaten with a little salt until they stuck to the dish, had been cooked by pouring quickly over them full-boiling water from a tea kettle. They hardly lost a bubble in the process—the water well drained away, the whites were ready to go on top of the custard in either bowls or goblets, and get themselves ornamented with crimson jelly, or flecks of cherry preserves. Like syllabub, boiled custard necessitated spoons—hence the borrowing of small silver was in most cases imperative. Plutocrats had not then been invented—but tradition tells of one high gentleman, who was self-sufficient. The fact stood him in good stead later—when he was darkly accused, she who had baked cakes for all his merry-makings said stoutly: "The Colonel do sech as that! Lord in heaven! Why, don't you know, in all the years I've knowed him, *he never had to borrow a single silver spoon*—and I've seen five hundred folks there for supper. I wouldn't believe them tales ef Angel Gabriel come down and told 'em to me."

Is anybody left, I wonder, who can cut oranges into lilies? Thus cut they surely looked pretty. The peel was divided evenly in six, the sections loosened, but not pulled free at the base. Instead the ends were curved backward after the manner of lily petals. The fruit, separated into eighths, hardly showed the divisions. These lilies sat flat upon the cloth, either in lines, as about square stacks, or around bigger things, or straight up and down the table center. They were not always in season—at their best around Christmas, but available until the end of winter.

Cheesecakes, baked in patty pans

frosted with cocoanut frosting, also helped
out the wedding richness. Indeed, guests
gathered to eat the fat and the sweet, no
less to drink it. Now, in a wider outlook,
I wonder a little if there was significance
in the fact that these wedding tables were
so void of color—showing only green and
white, with the tiniest sparks of red?

Party suppers had no such limitations—
often the table was gay with autumn leaves,
the center piece a riot of small ragged red
chrysanthemums, or raggeder pink or yellow ones, with candles glaring from gorgeous pumpkin jack-o'-lanterns down the
middle, or from the walls either side.
There were frosted cakes—loaves trimmed
gaily with red and white candies, or maybe
the frosting itself was tinted. In place of
syllabub or boiled custard, there were
bowls of ambrosia—oranges in sections,
freed of skin and seed, and smothered in
grated fresh cocoanut and sugar. Often
the bowl-tops were ornamented with leaves
cut deftly from the skin of deep red apples,
and alternating, other leaves shaped from
orange peel. Christmas party suppers

had touches of holly and cedar, but there was no attempt to match the elaborate wedding tables. Hog's foot jelly, red with the reddest wine, came in handily for them —since almost every plantation had a special small hog-killing, after the middle of December, so there might be fresh backbones, spare ribs, sausage and souse to help make Christmas cheer. Ham, spiced and sliced wafer thin, was staple for such suppers—chicken and turkey appeared oftenest as salad, hot coffee, hot breads in variety, crisp celery, and plenteous pickle, came before the sweets. Punch, not very heady, hardly more than a fortified pink lemonade, came with the sweets many times. Grandfather's punch was held sacred to very late suppers, hot and hearty, set for gentlemen who had played whist or euchre until cock-crow.

These are but indications. Fare varied even as did households and occasions. But everywhere there was kinship of the underlying spirit—which was the concrete expression of hospitality in good cheer. There was little luxury—rather we lived

amid a spare abundance, eating up what
had no market—I recall clearly times when
you could hardly give away fresh eggs, or
frying-size chickens, other times when eggs
fetched five cents for two dozen—provided
the seller would "take it in trade." Chickens then, broiling size, were forty to fifty
cents the dozen—with often an extra one
thrown in for good measure. For then
chicken cholera had not been invented—at
least not down in the Tennessee blue grass
country. Neither had hog cholera—nor
railroads. All three fell upon us a very
little before the era of the Civil War.
Steamboats ran almost half the year, but
the flat boat traffic had been taken away by
the peopling prairies, which could raise
so much more corn, derivatively so many
more hogs, to the man's work. Money
came through wheat and tobacco—not lav-
ishly, yet enough for our needs. All this
is set forth in hope of explaining in some
measure, the cookery I have tried to write
down faithfully—with so much of everything in hand, stinting would have been
sinful.

There was barbecue, and again there were barbecues. The viand is said to get its name from the French phrase *a barbe d' ecu,* from tail to head, signifying that the carcass was cooked whole. The derivation may be an early example of making the punishment fit the crime. As to that I do not know. What I do know is that lambs, pigs, and kids, when barbecued, are split in half along the backbone. The animals, butchered at sundown, and cooled of animal heat, after washing down well, are laid upon clean, split sticks of green wood over a trench two feet deep, and a little wider, and as long as need be, in which green wood has previously been burned to coals. There the meat stays twelve hours —from midnight to noon next day, usually. It is basted steadily with salt water, applied with a clean mop, and turned over once only. Live coals are added as needed from the log fire kept burning a little way off. All this sounds simple, dead-easy. Try it —it is really an art. The plantation barbecuer was a person of consequence— moreover, few plantations could show a master of the art. Such an one could give himself lordly airs—the loan of him was an act of special friendship—profitable always to the personage lent. Then as now there were free barbecuers, mostly white —but somehow their handiwork lacked a little of perfection. For one thing, they never found out the exact secret of "dipney," the sauce that savored the meat when it was crisply tender, brown all over, but free from the least scorching.

Daddy made it thus: Two pounds sweet lard, melted in a brass kettle, with one pound beaten, not ground, black pepper, a pint of small fiery red peppers, nubbed and stewed soft in water to barely cover, a spoonful of herbs in powder—he would never tell what they were,—and a quart and pint of the strongest apple vinegar, with a little salt. These were simmered together for half an hour, as the barbecue was getting done. Then a fresh, clean mop was dabbed lightly in the mixture, and as lightly smeared over the upper sides of the carcasses. Not a drop was permitted to fall on the coals—it would have sent up smoke, and films of light ashes. Then, tables being set, the meat was laid, hissing hot, within clean, tight wooden trays, deeply gashed upon the side that had been next the fire, and deluged with the sauce, which the mop-man smeared fully over it.

Hot! After eating it one wanted to lie down at the spring-side and let the water of it flow down the mouth. But of a flavor, a savor, a tastiness, nothing else earthly approaches. Not food for the gods, perhaps, but certainly meat for *men*. Women loved it no less—witness the way they begged for a quarter of lamb or shoat or kid to take home. The proper accompaniments to barbecue are sliced cucumbers in strong vinegar, sliced tomatoes, a great plenty of salt-rising light bread—and a greater plenty of cool ripe watermelons, by way of dessert.

So much for barbecue edible. Barbecue, the occasion, has yet to be set forth. Its First Cause was commonly political—the old south loved oratory even better than the new. Newspapers were none so plenty —withal of scant circulation. Besides,

reading them was work—also tedious and
tasteless. So the great and the would-be
great, rode up and down, and roundabout,
mixing with the sovereigns, and enlighten-
ing the world. Each party felt honor
bound to gather the sovereigns so they
might listen in comfort. Besides—they
wanted amusement—a real big barbecue
was a sort of social exchange, drawing together half of three counties, and letting
you hear and tell, things new, strange, and
startling. Furthermore, it was no trouble
to get carcasses—fifty to a hundred was not
uncommon. Men, women, children, everybody, indeed, came. The women brought
bread and tablecloths, and commonly much
beside. There was a speaker's stand, flag
draped—my infant eyes first saw the Stars
and Stripes floating above portraits—al-
leged—of Filmore and Buchanan, in the
campaign of '56. That meant the barbecue was a joint affair—Whigs and Demo-
crats getting it up, and both eagerly ready
to whoop it up for their own speakers.
Naturally in that latitude, Fremont was
not even named. No court costume with a

tail three yards long, could to-day make me feel one-half so fine as the white jaconet, and green sash then sported.

It was said there were a thousand at the barbecue. The cheering, at its loudest, was heard two miles away. To me it seemed as though all the folk in the world had gathered in that shady grove—I remember wondering if there could possibly be so many watermelons, some would be left for the children. Four big wagon loads lay bobbing in the coolth of the spring branch. It was a very cold spring with mint growing beside it, as is common with springs thereabout. Early settlers planted it thus hard by the water—they built their houses high, and water got warm in carrying it up hill. Lacking ice houses, to have cool juleps, they had to be mixed right at the well-head. Sugar, spoons, goblets, and the jug, were easily carried down there.

Juleps were not mixed openly that day —but the speakers had pitchers full of something that seemed to refresh their eloquence, no less than themselves. They hammered each other lustily, cheered to the echo by uproarious partisans, from nine in the morning until six in the afternoon. Luckily for them, there were four of them, thus they could ''spell' each other—and the audience. I did not mind them—not in the least. How should I—when right in front of me sat a lady with the most gorgeous flowers upon her white chip bonnet, and one beside me, who insisted upon my wearing, until time to go home, her watch and chain?

The watermelons held out—we took two big ones home to Mother, also a lot of splendid Indian peaches, and a fore-quarter of lamb. Mother rarely went out, being an invalid—so folk vied with each other in sending her things. I mention it, only by way of showing there were things to be sent, even after feeding the multitude. The black people went away full fed, and full handed—nobody who carried a basket had much relish for taking home again any part of its contents.

Our countryside's cooking came to its full flower for the bran-dances—which came into being, I think, because the pioneers liked to shake limber heels, but had not floors big enough for the shaking. So in green shade, at some springside they built an arbor of green boughs, leveled the earth underneath, pounded it hard and smooth, then covered it an inch deep with clean wheat bran, put up seats roundabout it, also a fiddlers' stand, got the fiddlers, printed invitations which went far and wide to women young and old, saw to a sufficiency of barbecue, depended on the Lord and the ladies for other things—and prepared to dance, dance from nine in the morning until two next morning. Men were not specifically invited—anybody in good standing with a clean shirt, dancing shoes, a good horse and a pedigree, was heartily welcome. The solid men, whose names appeared as managers, paid scot for everything—they left the actual arrangements to the lads. But they came in shoals to the bran-dances, and were audacious enough often to take away from some youth fathoms deep in love, his favorite partner. Sometimes, too, a lot of them pre-empted all the prettiest girls, and danced a special set with them. Thus were they delivered into the hands of the oppressed—the lads made treaty with the fiddlers and prompter to play fast and furious—to call figures that kept the oldsters wheeling and whirling. It was an endurance contest—but victory did not always perch with the youths. Plenty of pursy gentlemen were still light enough on their feet, clear enough in their wind, to dance through Money Musk double, Chicken in the Bread Tray, and the Arkansaw Traveller, no matter what the time.

All dances were square—quadrilles and cotillions. The Basket Cotillion was indeed, looked upon as rather daring. You see, at the last, the ring of men linked by hand-hold outside a ring of their partners, lifted locked arms over their partners' heads, and thus interwoven, the circle balanced before breaking up. Other times, other dances—ours is now the day of the trot and the tango. But they lack the life, the verve of the old dances, the old tunes. To this day when I hear them, my feet pat-

ter in spite of me. You could not dance
to them steadily, with soft airs blowing all
about, leaves flittering in sunshine, and
water rippling near, without getting an
appetite commensurate to the feasts in
wait for you.

One basket from a plantation sufficed for
bran-dances ending at sundown—those running on past midnight demanded two. It
would never do to offer snippets and fragments for supper. Barbecue, if there were
barbecue—was merely a concomitant of the
feeding, not the whole thing. Part of it
was left untouched to help out with supper.
So were part of the melons, and much of
the fruit. Apples, pears and peaches were
plenty in good years—the near plantations
sent them by wagon loads—as they also
sent ice cream by freezerfuls, and boilers
to make coffee. These were dispensed
more than generously—but nobody would
have helped himself to them uninvited, any
more readily than he would have helped
himself to money in the pocket. All that
was in the baskets was spread on the general tables, but no man thought of eating

thereof, until all women and children had been served. Old men came next—the women generally forcing upon them the best of everything.

Such a best! Broiled chicken, fried chicken, in quantity, whole hams simply entreating to be sliced, barbecue, pickle in great variety, drained and sliced for eating, beaten biscuit, soda biscuit, egg bread, salt-rising bread, or rolls raised with hop-yeast—only a few attempted them—every manner of pie, tart, and tartlet that did not drip and mess things, all the cakes in the calendar of good housewifery—with, now and then, new ones specially invented. Even more than a wedding, a bran-dance showed and proved your quality as a cake-maker. Cakes were looked at in broad daylight, eaten not with cloyed finicky appetites, but with true zest. Woe and double woe to you if a loaf of pride showed at cutting a "sad" streak, not quite done. Joy untold if you were a raw young house-keeper, to have your cake acclaimed by eaters and critics.

Mammy, and other Mammies, moved

proudly about, each a sort of oracle to the friends of her household. They kept sharp eyes on things returnable—plates, platters, knives, spoons, and tablecloths—in any doubtful case, arising from the fact of similarity in pattern, they were the court of last resort. Spoons and so on are unmistakable—but one sprigged saucer is very like other saucers sprigged the same. It was the Mammies rather than the masters and mistresses, who ordered carriage drivers and horse boys imperiously about. But nobody minded the imperiousness—it was no day for quarrelling or unwisdom. And it would surely have been unwise to fret those who were the Keepers of the Baskets, at the very last.

After dinner one went to the dressing-room, a wide roofless space enclosed with green boughs massed on end, and furnished plentifully with water in buckets, towels, basins, pin cushions, combs and brushes, face powder, even needles and thread. Thence one emerged after half an hour quite fresh—to dance on and on, till the fiddlers played a fast finale, and went to their supper. Then came an interval of talk and laughing, of making new friends or stabbing delicately old enemies. Also and further much primping in the dressing-room. Dancing steadily through a temperature of 98 in the shade plays hob with some sorts of prettiness. But as dew fell and lighted lanterns went up about the arbor and throughout the grove, supper was very welcome. There was hot coffee for everybody, likewise milk, likewise lemonade, with buttered biscuit, chicken, ham, and barbecue. Chicken-loaf was particularly good for such uses. To make it, several plump, tender, full-grown pullets were simmered in water to barely cover them, with a few pepper corns, half a dozen cloves, and a blade of mace, until very, very tender. Then the meat was picked from the bones, cut up while still hot, packed down in something deep, seasoning it to taste with salt, as it was packed, and dusting in more pepper if needed, then the liquor which had been kept at a brisk boil was poured over, and left to cool. No bother about skimming off fat—we liked our loaf rich as well as high-flavored. It came out a fine mottled solid that could be sliced thin, and eaten delicately between the halves of a buttered biscuit. Sandwiches were known—but only in books. Which was well—they would have dried out so badly, for this was before the era of wax paper. Since everything was packed in the baskets whole, there was much work for mothers and Mammies at the unpacking and table-setting.

Tarts, especially if filled with cheesecake or jelly custard, held high place among the sweets. Especially with the men, young and old. One, a manager, who had been here, there, everywhere, since eight o'clock in the morning, asked Mammy at suppertime to: "Please save him one more dozen of them little pies." In truth the little pies made no more than a mouthful for noble appetites. Pies, full-grown, did not go begging—and were seldom cut in less than quarters. Frosted cake—which the lads denominated "whitewashed," was commonly saved over for the supper baskets. It kept moist, whereas without the frosting a long summer day might make it hard.

After the supper elderly men drove home—unless they had daughters among the dancers without other chaperons. Generally, some aunt or cousin stood ready with such good offices. The chaperons themselves danced now and then—youths specially anxious for favor with their charges, all but forced them upon the floor. Set it to their credit, they footed it almost as lightly as the youngest. Occasionally you might see, mother and daughter, even a granddaughter of tender years, wheeling and balancing in the same set. And so the fiddles played, the stars shone, the waters babbled, until the lanterns flared and sputtered out, and the banjo-picker held up fingers raw and bleeding. Then with a last final swing and flourish, everybody scattered for homeward ways, glad of the day's pleasure—and tired enough to be glad also it was ended.

The most special of occasions was a dining. Not upon any high day or holiday, such as Christmas, New Year, Jackson's

Day—the eighth of January—Easter nor Whit-Monday, but as Mammy said: "A dinin' des, dry so." Commonly pride of housewifery incited to it—therefore it must be a triumph. The hour was two o'clock, but guests came around eleven or twelve—and spent the day. They sat down to tables that well might have groaned, even howled, such was the weight they carried. Twelve was a favorite guest-number—few tables could be stretched to hold more than twelve plates. There were but two courses—dinner and dessert—unless in very cold weather, some person who would nowadays be said to be fond of putting on frills, set before her guests, plates of steaming soup. It had to smell very good, else it was no more than tasted—folk did not care to dull the edge of appetite needlessly, with so much before them. For the table was fully set—a stuffed ham at one end, a chicken or partridge pie at the other, side dishes of smothered rabbit, or broiled chicken, at least four kinds of sweet pickle, as many of jelly and sour pickle, a castor full of catsups, tomato and

walnut, plain vinegar, pepper vinegar, red
and black pepper, and made mustard, all
the vegetables in season—I have seen corn
pudding, candied sweet potatoes, Irish potatoes, mashed and baked, black-eyed peas,
baked peaches, apples baked in sugar and
cloves, cabbage boiled with bacon, okra,
stewed tomatoes, sliced raw tomatoes, cucumbers cut up with young onions, beets
boiled and buttered, and string beans,
otherwise snaps, all at one spread.

Only epicures dressed their lettuce at
table.   One cranky old family friend had
it served to him in a water bucket, set beside him on the floor.   He shook it free of
water, cut it, without bruising, to wide
ribbons, covered them thickly with hard-
boiled egg-yolk mashed fine, then poured
upon it clear ham gravy, and strong vinegar, added salt and pepper, black and red
—then ate his fill.   But, of course, he did
not do that at dinings.   For then, if lettuce appeared, it was cut up, dressed with
vinegar, salt, sugar, and pepper, but guilt-
less of oil, garnished with rings of hard-
boiled egg—and very generally, and justly,

neglected. Still the hostess had the satisfaction of feeling she had offered it—that she had indeed offered more than could have been reasonably expected.

There was water to drink, also cider in season, also milk, sweet and sour, and the very best of the homemade wine. Decanters of it sat up and down the table—you could fill up and come again at pleasure. The one drawback was—it was hard to eat properly, when you were so interrupted by helpings to something else. If there was a fault in our old-time cooking, it was its lack of selection. I think those who gave dinings felt uneasy if there was unoccupied room for one more dish.

Dessert was likewise an embarrassment of riches. Cakes in variety, two sorts of pie, with ice cream or sherbet, or fresh fruit, did not seem too much to those dear Ladies Bountiful. There was no after-dinner coffee. In cold weather coffee in big cups, with cream and sugar, often went with the main dinner. Hot apple toddies preceded it at such times. In hot weather the precursor was mint julep, ice cold.

Yet we were not a company of dyspeptics nor drunkards—by the free and full use of earth's abounding mercies we learned not to abuse them.

Birthday Barbecue: (Dorothy Dix.) As refined gold can be gilded, barbecue, common, or garden variety, can take on extra touches. As thus: Kill and dress quickly a fine yearling wether, in prime condition but not over-fat, sluice out with cool water, wipe dry inside and out with a soft, damp cloth, then while still hot, fill the carcass cram-full of fresh mint, the tenderer and more lush the better, close it, wrap tight in a clean cloth wrung very dry from cold salt water, then pop all into a clean, bright tin lard stand, with a tight-fitting top, put on top securely, and sink the stand head over ears in cold water —a spring if possible. Do this around dusk and leave in water until very early morning. Build fire in trench of hard wood logs before two o'clock. Let it burn to coals—have a log fire some little way off to supply fresh coals at need. Lay a breadth of galvanized chicken-wire—large

mesh—over the trench. Take out carcass—split it half down back bone, lay it
flesh side down, on the wire grid, taking
care coals are so evenly spread there is
no scorching. After an hour begin basting with "the sop." It is made thus.
Best butter melted, one pound, black pepper ground, quarter pound, red pepper
pods, freed of stalk and cut fine to almost
a paste, half a pint, strong vinegar, scant
pint, brandy, peach if possible though
apple or grape will answer, half a pint.
Cook all together over very slow heat or
in boiling water, for fifteen minutes. The
sop must not scorch, but the seasoning
must be cooked through it. Apply with
a big soft swab made of clean old linen,
but not old enough to fray and string.
Baste meat constantly. Put over around
four in the morning, the barbecue should
be done, and well done, by a little after
noon. There should be enough sop left to
serve as gravy on portions after it is
helped. The meat, turned once, has a
fine crisped surface, and is flavored all
through with the mint, and seasoning.

Soap and Candles

Dip-candles I never saw in common use
—but Mammy showed me how they were
made back at Ole Marster's, in the days
when candle-molds were not to be had.
Dipped or molded, the candles were of
varying substance. Tallow was the main
reliance—mutton tallow as well as that
from our beeves. It was tried out fresh,
and hardened with alum in the process.
The alum was dissolved in a little water,
and put with the raw fat as it went over
the fire. By and by the water all cooked
away, leaving the alum well incorporated
through the clear fat. Lacking it, a little

clear lye went in—Mammy thought and
said, the lye ate up the oil in the tallow,
making it firmer and whiter. But lye and
alum could not go in at the same time,
since being alkaline and acid, they would
destroy each other.

Great pains were taken not to scorch
the tallow—that meant smelly and ill-col-
ored candles. After straining it clear of
cracklings, it was caked in something deep,
then turned out and laid on the highest
shelf in the lumber house to await molding time. Cakes of beeswax were kept in
the Jackson press, so children, white and
black, could not take bites for chewing.
It ranked next to native sweet gum for
such uses—but Mammy felt it had much
better be saved to mix with the tallow at
melting time. It made the candles much
firmer, also bettered their light, and moreover changed the tallow hue to an agree-
able very pale yellow. Bee hives, like
much else, were to a degree primitive—the
wax came from comb crushed in the straining of honey. It was boiled in water to
take away the remnant sweetness, then

allowed to cool on top the water, taken
off, and remelted over clean water, so
manipulated as to free it from foreign
substances, then molded into cakes. One
cake was always set apart for the neighborhood cobbler, who melted it with
tallow and rosin to make shoemaker's
wax. Another moiety was turned into
grafting wax—by help of it one orchard
tree bore twelve manners of fruit. And
still another, a small, pretty cake from
a scalloped patty pan, found place in
the family work basket—in sewing by
hand with flax thread, unless you waxed it,
it lost strength, and quickly pulled to
pieces.

We bought our flax thread in skeins, but
Mammy loved to tell of spinning it back
in the days when she was young, and the
best spinner on the old plantation. She
still spun shoe-thread for her friend the
cobbler, who, however, furnished her the
raw flax, which he had grown, rotted and
hechtelled, in his bit of bottom land. There
were still spinning and weaving in plenty
at our house—Mother had made, yearly,

jeans, linsey, carpets and so on—but the plantation was not wholly clothed with homespun, as had been the case in her father's house.

Return we to our candle-making. It was work for the very coldest weather— even though we had two sets of molds, needs must the candles harden quickly if the making was to speed well. Molds could be filled at the kitchen hearth, then set outside to cool. For dipping the tallow-pot had to be set over an outside fire, and neighbored by a ladder, laid flat on trestles with smooth boards laid underneath. Mammy spun the candle wicks— from long-staple cotton, drawing it out thick, and twisting it barely enough to hold together. It must not be too coarse, as it had to be doubled over reeds at top, either for molding or dipping.

The molds were of candle-shape, joined in batteries of six or twelve, with a pert handle at one side, and tiny holes at the tips, through which the wick-ends were thrust, by help of a long broom-straw. Well in place they were drawn taut, the reeds so placed as to hold the wicks centrally, then tallow melted with beeswax, in due proportion, was poured around till the molds were brim full—after which they were plunged instantly into a tub of cold water standing outside. This to prevent oozings from the tip—hot grease is the most insidious of all substances. Only in zero weather would the first oozings harden enough to plug the orifice quickly. When the candles had hardened properly, the mold was either held over the fire, or thrust in hot water half a minute, then the candles withdrawn by help of the reeds. They were cooled a bit, to save the softened outside, then nubbed of surplus wick, and laid in a dish outside. Careless or witless molders, by laying candles still soft upon the pile, often made themselves double work.

Tallow for dipping, was kept barely fluid, by setting it over embers a little way off the fire. The pot had to be deep, so the wicks could be sunk in it to full length. They were thus sunk by stickfuls, lifted up quickly, and hung between the ladder rungs to drip. Half the tallow on them dripped away—indeed, after the first dipping they looked little more than clotted ghosts of themselves in their last estate. In very cold weather three drippings sufficed— otherwise there must be four or five. Since the dip was the result of cooled accretions, it was always top-heavy—much bigger at the nose than the base. A quick and skilled worker, though, could dip a hundred candles in the time required to mold two dozen. They burned out so quickly that was a crowning mercy—half a dozen was the average of a long winter evening. Further they ran down, in great masses— hence the importance of saving up drippings. Even molded candles made them plentiful enough to be worth re-molding. This unless discolored with the brass of candlesticks—in that case their last end was soap grease.

Rush lights were dips—this I state on information and belief, since I never saw one. Also on information and belief, it is here set forth, that folk in the back countries where wicking was not easily had, used instead of wicks, splinters of fat pine, known as light wood. In proof, take Candle Wood Mountain, whose name is said to have come from furnishing such fat pine, and of a special excellence. The pine splinters must, I think, have given a better light than real wicks—my father, in Tennessee, never ceased sighing for the lightwood, which had made such cheery illumination back in his boyhood, in a Carolina home.

Every sort of waste fat became at the last, soap grease. Bones even were thrown into kettles of lye, which ate out all their richness, leaving them crumbly, and fit for burying about the grapevines. Hence the appositeness of the darkey saying, to express special contempt of a suitor: "My Lawd! I wouldn't hab dat nigger, not eben for soap grease." Which has always seemed to me, in a way, a classic of condemnation.

Soap making came twice a year—the main event in March, to get free of things left over from hog killing, the supplement in September or October, to use up sum-

mer savings. Each was preceded by dripping lye. This necessitated wood ashes,
of course—ashes from green wood. Oak
or hickory was best. They were kept dry
until they went into hoppers, where they
were rotted by gentle wetting for a space
of several days. Then water was dripped
through, coming out a dark brown caustic
liquid, clean-smelling, but ill to handle—
it would eat a finger-tip carelessly thrust
in it to the raw.

But even thus it was not strong enough
for proper soapmaking, so it was boiled,
boiled, until it would eat a feather, merely
drawn quickly through it. Grease was
added then, a little at a time, and stirred
well through, changing the black-brown
lye into a light-brown, bubbly mass.
Whatever the lye would not eat of the
grease's components, was skimmed out
with the big perforated ladle. Even beyond candle-molding, soap-making was
an art. Mammy never would touch it,
until "the right time of the moon." Also
and further, she used a sassafras stick for
stirring, put it in the first time with her

right hand, and always stirred the kettle the same way. If a left-handed person came near the kettle she was mightily vexed—being sure her soap would go wrong. She kept on the fire beside it a smaller kettle of clear lye, to be added at need, without checking the boiling.

Boiling down lye took one day, boiling in grease another. The third morning, after the fire was well alight, she tested the soap, by making a bit into lather. If the lather were clean and clear, without a film of grease on top, she knew it remained only to cook the soap down thick enough for the barrel, or to make into balls by the addition of salt. But if the film appeared —then indeed there was trouble. First aid to it was more lye, of feather-eating strength—next a fresh sassafras stirring stick, last and most important, walking backwards as she put the stick in the kettle, though she would never admit she did this on purpose. Like the most of her race she was invincibly shy about acknowledging her beliefs in charms and conjuring.

Soap which failed to thicken properly

lacked grease. To put in enough, yet not too much, was a matter of nice judgment. Tallow did not mix well with hog fat. Therefore it had commonly its smaller special pot, whose results were molded for hand-soap, being hard and rather light-colored.

Since our washerwomen much preferred soft soap, most of the spring making went straight into the barrel. The barrel had to be very tight—soap has nearly as great a faculty of creeping through seams as even hot lard. One kettleful, however, would have salt stirred through it, then be allowed to cool, and be cut out in long bars, which were laid high and dry to age. Old soap was much better for washing fine prints, lawns, ginghams and so on—in fact whatever needed cleansing without fading.

Sundry other fine soap makers emptied their salted soap, just as it was on the point of hardening, into shallow pans, cloth-lined, and shaped it with bare hands into balls the size of two fists. This they did with the whole batch, holding hard soap so much easier kept, and saying it was no

trouble whatever to soften a ball in a little
hot water upon wash days. But Mammy
would have none of such practices—said
give her good soft soap and sand rock, she
could scour anything. Sand rock was a
variety of limestone, which burning made
crumbly, but did not turn to lime. Mammy
picked it up wherever she found it, beat it
fine and used it on everything—shelves,
floors, hollow-ware, milk pans, piggins,
cedar water buckets—it made their brass
hoops shine like gold. While she scoured
she told us tales of the pewter era—when
she had gone, a barefoot child, with her
mother, to the Rush Branch, to come home
with a sheaf of rushes, whereby the pewter
was made to shine. It hurts even yet, recalling the last end of that pewter. As
glass and crockery grew plenty, the boys
—my uncles, there were five of them—
melted it down for rifle bullets, when by
chance they ran out of lead. Yet—who
am I, to reproach them—did not I myself,
melt down for a purpose less legitimate a
fine Brittania ware teapot, whose only

fault was a tiny leak? Now I should prize it beyond silver and gold.

Harking back to candle-making—we had no candle-berries in our wilds, and only a few wax-berries as ornaments of our gardens. But from what I know by observation and experience, the candle-berries or bayberries, can be melted in hot water, the same as honey-comb, and the wax strained away from the seedy residue, then allowed to cool, on top the water, and clarified by a further melting and cooling over water. Mixed with paraffine it can be molded into real bayberry candles, ever so much more odorous than those of commerce. It is well to remember in buying paraffine that there are three qualities of it, differing mainly in the degree of heat at which they melt. Choose that which is hardest to melt for candle-making. One might indeed, experiment with bayberry wax, and the drippings of plain paraffine candles, before undertaking candle-making to any considerable extent.

A last word. If any incline to challenge things here set forth, will they please remember that as one star differs from another in glory, so does one family, one region, differ from all others in its manners of eating, drinking, and cooking. I have written true things, but make no claim that they apply all over. Indeed there may be those to whom they will seem a transversing of wisdom and experience. To all such I say, try them intelligently, with pains and patience, and of the results, hold fast to that you find good.

INDEX

DRINKS

EGGS